FOURTH EDITION

EXERCISES IN HELPING SKILLS
A Training Manual to Accompany The Skilled Helper

D0731646

EXERCISES IN HELPING SKILLS
A Training Manual to Accompany The Skilled Helper

Gerard Egan
Loyola University of Chicago

Brooks/Cole Publishing Company
Pacific Grove, California

Brooks/Cole Publishing Company
A Division of Wadsworth, Inc.

Printed in the United States of America

10   9   8   7   6   5   4   3   2

ISBN 0-534-12139-X

Sponsoring Editor: **Claire Verduin**
Marketing Representative: **Thomas L. Braden**
Editorial Assistant: **Gay C. Bond**
Production Editor: **Ellen Brownstein**
Cover Design and Illustration: **Roy R. Neuhaus**
Art Coordinator: **Cloyce J. Wall**
Cover Printing: **Phoenix Color Corp.**
Printing and Binding: **Malloy Lithographing**

CONTENTS

PART ONE

INTRODUCTION

The exercises in this manual are meant to accompany the revised edition of **THE SKILLED HELPER** by Gerard Egan (Brooks/Cole Publishing Company, Pacific Grove, California, 1990). These exercises serve a number of purposes:

1. They can help you develop a **behavioral** rather than merely a cognitive grasp of the principles, skills, and methods that turn helping models into useful tools.
2. They can be used to help you explore your own strengths and weaknesses as a helper. That is, they provide a way of having you apply the helping model to **yourself** first before trying it out on others. As such, they can help you confirm strengths that enable you to be with clients effectively and manage weaknesses that would stand in the way of helping clients manage problem situations.
3. You can help **clients** use these exercises selectively to explore and manage their own problems in living more effectively. These exercises provide one way of promoting client participation in the helping process.
4. You can help clients use these exercises to learn the **skills of problem management** themselves. Training in problem-management skills encourages self-responsibility in clients and helps make them less dependent on others in managing their lives.

A TRAINING PROGRAM FOR HELPERS

The following are standard steps in a skills-training program:

1. First, develop a **cognitive understanding** of a particular helping method or the skill of delivering it. You can do this by reading the text and listening to lectures.

2. **Clarify** what you have read or heard. This can be done through instructor-led questioning and discussion.

The objective of Steps 1 and 2 is **cognitive clarity.**

3. Watch experienced instructors **model** the skill or method in question. This can be done "live" or through films and videotapes.

4. **Use** the skill or method you have read about and seen demonstrated. The first "use" of a skill may be doing an exercise in this manual. The purpose of this initial use of the method or skill is to demonstrate to yourself that you understand the helping method or skill enough to begin to practice it.

The objective of Steps 3 and 4 is **behavioral clarity.**

5. Move into smaller groups to **practice** the skill or method in question with your fellow trainees.

6. During these practice sessions evaluate your own performance and get **feedback** from a trainer and from your fellow trainees. This feedback serves to confirm what you are doing right and to correct what you are doing wrong. The use of video to provide feedback is most helpful.

The objective of Steps 5 and 6 is <u>initial competence</u> in using the model and the skills that make it work.

7. Finally, from time to time stop and reflect on the training process itself. Take the opportunity to express how you feel about the training process and how you feel about your own progress. While Steps 1 through 6 deal with the task of learning the helping model and the methods and skills that make it work, Step 7 deals with group maintenance, that is, managing the needs of individual trainees. Doing this kind of group maintenance work helps establish a learning community.

The exercises in this manual can be used as a way of practicing the skills and methods "in private" before practicing them with your fellow trainees. They provide a behavioral link between the introduction to a skill or method that takes place in the first four steps of this training format and actual practice in a group.

THE STAGES AND STEPS OF THE HELPING PROCESS

For the most part the exercises presented here are grouped around and follow the order of the three stages and nine steps of the helping process. Here is an outline of the skilled-helper model.

STAGE I: EXPLORING THE PRESENT STATE OF AFFAIRS

Clients can neither manage problem situations nor develop unused opportunities unless they identify and understand them. Exploration and clarification of problems and opportunities take place in Stage I. This stage deals with the current state of affairs, that is, the problem situations or unused opportunities that prompt clients to come for help. This stage includes the following steps:

1. <u>**Help clients tell their stories.**</u> First of all, clients need to tell their stories. Some do so easily, others with a great deal of difficulty. You need to develop a set of attitudes and communication skills that will enable you to help clients reveal problems in living and unused potential. This means helping clients find out what's going wrong and what's going right in their lives. Successful assessment helps clients identify both problems and resources.

2. <u>**Help clients develop new perspectives.**</u> This means helping clients manage **blind spots**, that is, helping them see themselves, their concerns, and the contexts of their concerns more objectively. This enables clients to see more clearly not only their problems and unused opportunities, but also ways in which they want their lives to be different. Your ability to challenge clients humanely and effectively throughout the helping process is extremely important.

3. <u>**Help clients focus on significant concerns**.</u> This means helping clients identify their most important concerns, especially if they have a number of problems. Effective counselors help clients work on high-leverage issues, that is, issues that will make a difference in clients' lives. They also help clients spell out problem situations in terms of specific experiences, behaviors, and feelings.

STAGE II: DEVELOPING A PREFERRED SCENARIO

Once clients understand either problem situations or opportunities for development more clearly, they often need help in determining what they would like to see different. They need to develop a preferred scenario, that is, see a picture of a better future, choose specific goals to work on, and commit themselves to them. For instance, at this stage a troubled married couple could be helped to picture what a better marital relationship might look like.

1. **Help clients develop a range of possibilities for a better future.** If a client's current state of affairs is problematic and unacceptable, then he or she needs to be helped to conceptualize or envision a new state of affairs, that is, alternate, more acceptable possibilities. A new scenario is not a wild-eyed, idealistic state of affairs, but rather a conceptualization or a picture of what the problem situation would be like if improvements were made. For instance, for a couple whose marriage is coming apart and who fight constantly, one of the elements of the new scenario might be fewer and fairer fights. Other possible elements of this better marriage might be greater mutual respect, more openness, more effectively managed conflicts, a more equitable distribution of household tasks, and so forth. Separation or even divorce might be considered if differences are irreconcilable and if the couple's values system permits such a solution.

2. **Help clients translate preferred-scenario possibilities into goals.** Once a variety of preferred-scenario possibilities--which constitute possible goals or desired outcomes of the helping process--have been generated, it is time to help clients choose the possibilities that make the most sense and turn them into an agenda, that is, a goal or a "package" of goals to be accomplished. The agenda put together by the client needs to be viable, that is, capable of being translated into action. It is viable to the degree that it is stated in terms of clear and specific outcomes and is substantive or adequate, realistic, in keeping with the client's values, and capable of being accomplished within a reasonable time frame.

3. **Help clients commit themselves to the goals they choose.** Problem-managing goals are useless if they are not actively pursued by the client. Incentives for commitment to these goals must be discovered. The search for incentives is especially important when the choices are hard. How are truants with poor home situations to commit themselves to returning to school? What are the incentives for such a choice? Most clients struggle with commitment.

STAGE III: GETTING THERE--FORMULATING STRATEGIES AND PLANS

Discussing and evaluating preferred-scenario possibilities and choosing goals-- the work of Stage II--determine **what** must be accomplished by clients in order to manage their lives more effectively. Stage III deals with **how** goals are to be accomplished. Some clients know what they want to accomplish, but need help in determining how to do it. Throughout the counseling process rusty client imaginations need stimulating.

1. **Help clients brainstorm a range of strategies for accomplishing their goals.** In this step clients are helped to discover a number of different way of achieving their goals. The principle is simple: Action strategies tend to be more effective when chosen from among a number of possibilities. Some clients, when they decide what they want, leap into action, implementing the first strategy that comes to mind. While such a bias toward action may be laudable, the strategy may be ineffective, inefficient, imprudent, or a combination of all three.

2. **Help clients choose action strategies that best fit their resources.** If you do a good job in the first step of Stage III, that is, if you help clients identify a number of different ways of achieving their goals, then clients will face the task of choosing the best set. In this step your job is to help them choose the strategy or "package" of strategies that best fits their preferences and resources. This

3

tailoring of action strategies is important. One client might want to improve her interpersonal skills by taking a course at a college while another might prefer to work individually with a counselor.

3. **Help clients formulate a plan.** Once clients are helped to choose strategies that best fit their styles, resources, and environments, they need to assemble these strategies into a **plan**, a step-by-step process for accomplishing a goal. If a client has a number of goals, then the plan indicates the order in which they are to be pursued. Clients are more likely to act if they know what they need to do and the order they do it in. Plans help clients develop discipline and also keep them from being overwhelmed by the work they need to do.

CLIENT ACTION: THE HEART OF THE HELPING PROCESS

Help clients act both within and outside the counseling sessions. Helping is ultimately about problem-managing and opportunity-developing action. Discussions, analysis, goal setting, strategy formulation, and planning all make sense only to the degree that they help clients to act prudently and with direction. There is nothing magic about change; it is work. If clients do not act on their own behalf, nothing happens.

Two kinds of client action are important here: First, actions within the counseling sessions themselves. The nine steps described above are not things that helpers do to clients, rather they are things that clients are helped to do. Clients must take ownership of the helping process. Second, clients must act "out there" in their real day-to-day worlds. Problem-managing and opportunity-developing action is ultimately the name of the game. The stages and steps of the helping process, illustrated on the next page in Figure 1, make sense to the degree that they drive prudent client action.

Since all the stages and steps of the helping process can be drivers of client action, action themes will be woven into each set of exercises. This will reinforce the principle that discussion and action go hand in hand.

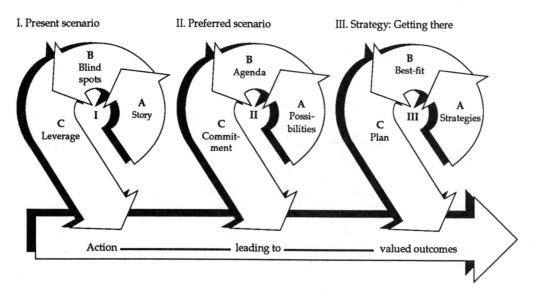

Figure 1. The Stages and Steps of the Helping Process

4

A NONLINEAR APPROACH TO HELPING

Helping usually does not take place in the neat, step-by-step fashion suggested by the stages and steps of the helping model. Effective helpers start wherever there is a client need. For instance, if a client needs support and challenge to commit himself or herself to realistic goals that have already been chosen, then the counselor tries to be helpful at this point. The nine steps of the helping model are active ways of being with clients in their attempts to manage problems in living and develop unused potential. You can be with clients in both supportive and challenging ways as they attempt to:

* tell their stories,
* deal with blind spots and develop new perspectives,
* choose issues to work on that will make a difference,
* develop a range of alternate scenarios,
* set realistic goals and agendas,
* commit themselves to these goals,
* develop a range of strategies for accomplishing goals,
* choose strategies that best fit their preferences and resources, and
* turn strategies into realistic action plans.

The needs of your clients and not the logic of a helping model should determine your interactions with them. One of the overriding needs of clients, of course, is to turn discussion and analysis of problem situations into problem-managing action. If you can help clients do this, you are worth your weight in gold.

YOUR ROLE AS TRAINEE: DEALING WITH REAL CONCERNS

One way of learning the stages and steps of this helping model is to apply them to your own problems and concerns first. This means placing yourself in the role of a client. There are two ways of doing this. You can pretend to be a client or you can really become a client. Since this distinction is important, let us look at it more carefully.

Role-playing versus dealing with real concerns. As a trainee, you are going to be asked to act both as helper and as client in practice sessions. In the written exercises in this manual, you are asked at one time or another to play each of these roles. There are two ways of playing the role of the client:

1. you can **role-play**, that is, pretend to have certain problems, or
2. you can discuss you own **real** problems and concerns.

Role-playing, while not easy, is still less personally demanding than discussing your own real concerns in practice sessions. Although some role-playing might be useful at the beginning of the training process (since it is less threatening and allows you to ease yourself into the role of client), I suggest that you eventually use the training process to look at some of the real problems or concerns in your own life, **especially issues that relate to your effectiveness as a helper**. For instance, if you tend to be an impatient person--one who places unreasonable demands on others--you will have to examine and change this behavior if you want to become an effective helper. Or, if you are very nonassertive, this may assist you in helping clients challenge themselves.

Learning what it means to be a client. Another reason for using real problems or concerns when you take the role of the client is that it gives you some experience of **being** a client. Then, when you face real clients, you can appreciate some of the misgivings they might have in talking to a relative stranger about the intimate details of their lives. Other things being equal, I would personally prefer going to a helper who has had some experience in being a client.

The safe and productive training group. Dealing with personal concerns in the training sessions will be both safe and productive if you have a competent trainer who provides adequate supervision, if the training group becomes a learning community that provides both support and reasonable challenge for its members, and if you are willing to discuss personal concerns. Self-disclosure will be counterproductive if you let others extort it from you or if you attempt to extort it from others. You self-disclosure should always remain appropriate to the goals of the training group. Extortion, "secret-dropping," and dramatic self-disclosure are counterproductive.

Preparing for self-disclosure. If you are to talk about yourself during the practice sessions, you should take some care in choosing what you are going to reveal about yourself. Making some preparation for what you are going to say can prevent you from revealing things about yourself that you would rather not. The exercises relating to Step I-A of the skilled-helper model will help you discover and explore the concerns that you can safely deal with in the training group.

SOME CAUTIONS IN USING THIS MANUAL

First, it is important to note that the exercises suggested in this manual are means, not ends in themselves. They are useful to the degree that they help you develop a working knowledge of the helping model and acquire the kinds of skills that will make you an effective helper. Other exercises can be added and the ones outlined here can be modified in order to achieve this goal more effectively.

Second, these exercises have been written as an adjunct to the text. They usually presuppose information in the text that is not repeated in the exercises.

Third, the length of training programs differs from setting to setting. In shorter programs there will not be time to do all these exercises. Nor is it necessary to do all of them. However, in shorter training programs, I suggest that you do at least one exercise from each of the sections on communication skills, one from each of the nine steps of the helping process, and one from the sections on action. This will help you develop a behavioral feeling for the **entire** helping model and not just the communication skills part of it. You will not know which parts of the helping model any given client will need until you sit down with him or her. If the entire focus of the training program is on the communication skills that serve the helping process, you should understand that your training is incomplete. Further training in the helping model itself is needed.

Fourth, these exercises achieve their full effect only if you share them with the members of your training group and receive **feedback** on how well you are learning the model and the skills that make it work. Your instructor will set up the structure needed to do this. Since time limitations are always an issue, learning how to give brief, concise, behavioral feedback in a humane, caring way is most important. Exercises on giving feedback are found in the communication skills section.

LEARNING JOURNAL

In many of the exercises you will be asked to jot down what you have learned about yourself, yourself in the role of helper, and yourself in the role of client. Many people find it very useful to jot these learnings down in a journal, which can be reviewed from time to time. It is one way of committing yourself to your own development as a human being and as a helper.

PART TWO

VALUES AND ACTION

Part Two deals with two areas of the helping process: The values that should permeate your interactions with your clients and the action orientation needed by clients in order to participate as fully as possible in the helping process and to manage the problems and opportunities of their lives more effectively.

I. Values. First, it is important for you to take initiative in determining the kinds of values you want to pervade the helping process and relationship. Too often such values are afterthoughts. The position taken in Chapter Three of the text is that values should provide guidance for everything you do in your interactions with clients.

II. Action Orientation. Second, since the skilled-helper model is action-oriented, it is important for you to understand the place of "getting things done" in your own life. If you are to be a catalyst for problem-managing and opportunity-developing action on the part of clients, then reviewing your own track record in this regard is important.

I. VALUES IN HELPING RELATIONSHIPS

As indicated in the text, the values that are to permeate your helping relationships and practice must be owned by you. Learning about values from others is very important, but mindless adoption of the values promoted by the helping profession without reflection inhibits your owning and practicing them. You need to wrestle with your values a bit to make them your own. Second, your values must actually make a difference in your interactions with clients. That is, they must be values-in-use and not merely espoused values. Your clients will get a feeling for your values, not from what you say, but from what you do.

EXERCISE 1: ADOPTING VALUES THAT BENEFIT CLIENTS

1. Put yourself in the shoes of the client. Without thinking of values, simply ask yourself: "What do I want to get out of seeing a helper? How do I want to be treated?" Then list what you want, using simple words and phrases rather than sentences.

_____ _____ _____

_____ _____ _____

_____ _____ _____

_____ _____ _____

_____ _____ _____

_____ _____ _____

_____ _____ _____

_____ _____ _____

2. Read the section on values in the text. See how many of the things you would want as a client fall under the values categories outlined in Chapter Three. List them under the following headings.

Helper Competence   **Helping Pragmatism**   **Respect for Client**

_____ _____ _____

_____ _____ _____

_____ _____ _____

_____ _____ _____

_____ _____ _____

_____ _____ _____

_____ _____ _____

Helper Genuineness   **Client Self-Responsibility**

_____ _____

_____ _____

_____ _____

_____ _____

_____ _____

_____   _____

_____   _____

_____   _____

3. Star those words or phrases that you consider to represent **key** values in the helping process and relationship.

4. What do you need to do to make sure that the values you have starred actually permeate your interactions with clients?

EXERCISE 2: SHARING KEY HELPING VALUES WITH CO-LEARNERS

Do [illegible] friends

1. Make copies of the values you have highlighted for yourself in the previous exercise. Share them with the other members of your small group.

2   Through discussion and debate, work together to produce a "Key Helping Values" list for your group.

3. Finally, in an open session, share your group's list with the other groups.

4. Discuss the differences among the groups and the implications for helping. What value themes emerge? Are there significant differences among the groups? What do you learn from these themes and these differences?

Obviously Chapter Three and these two exercises do not take care of your education on values in helping relationships. They are meant to help you start the long-term process of seeing helping from a values perspective. Values at their most pragmatic are criteria that help you make decisions. Throughout the training program values issues will arise. Your instructor will help you work through these.

II. ACTION ORIENTATION

Unfortunately, helping often suffers from too much talking and not enough doing. Research shows that helpers are sometimes more interested in getting clients to develop new insights than in acting on them. Part of this stems from the fact that not all of us are as proactive in managing the problems and opportunities of our own lives as we might be. Inertia and procrastination plague most of us. The exercises in this section are designed to help you explore your own orientation toward action so that you may become a more effective stimulus to action for your clients.

EXERCISE 3: EXPLORING YOUR ACTION ORIENTATION

1. Read Chapter Four in the text, which deals with blocks to action.
2. Identify one way in which you chronically put off action.
3. Identify one project that you have been putting off.

Example

Dahlia, 55, whose children are now grown, has returned to school in order to become a counselor. She has this to say about her action orientation.

Chronic Procrastination Scenario

"My husband is in business for himself. I take care of a lot of the routine correspondence for the business and our household. Often I let it pile up. The more it piles up the more I hate to face it. On occasion, an important business letter gets lost in the shuffle. This annoys my husband a great deal. Then with a great deal of flurry, I do it all and for a while keep current. But then I slide back into my old ways. I also notice that when I let it pile up I waste a lot of time reading junk mail--catalogs of things I'm not going to buy, things like that."

A Project Being Put Off

"I have an older sister who is a widow. She has one autistic child, nearly 20 now, who is at home. He goes to a school for autistic citizens--it's not just kids--and is gone several hours every week day. Lately, he is becoming more difficult to manage. He has temper outbursts and things like that. This puts a great deal of stress on my sister. She's much more timid than I am. The day will come when she can no longer take care of him. I have told her that I would help her in the whole process of placing him in an institution of some kind. I know she can use my help. If I don't do anything, things will just get worse. One of my major concerns is ending up doing something _for_ my sister. I have to do whatever I'm going to do _with_ her. I've been putting off doing anything about it because I know it will be extremely difficult for her. It's not my favorite project. I think about it at least once a day, then I put it out of my mind."

4. Sit down with a partner and help one another answer the question: What's going on here? What can I learn about myself as a helper by reviewing the ways I avoid action in my own life?
5. In the full group, share one or two of your key learnings. Jot the key learnings down in your journal.

EXERCISE 4: WAYS OF IMPROVING YOUR ACTION ORIENTATION

Exercise 3 is about awareness. This exercise is about helping yourself become more proactive. It is about problem-managing action itself.

1. Take two sheets of paper. At the top of one write the words "Chronic Procrastination Scenario." At the top of the other, write "Delayed Project." Now that your awareness of both of these has been increased, write down as many actions as possible that you could take to manage each of these issues. Note that in the first you will be writing down patterns of behavior that need to be put in place and kept in place if you are to avoid chronic procrastination in that area of life. In the second you will be writing down specific actions you can take to move the project along.
2. Review both lists and star the items that you think would be most helpful in managing the problem.
3. Get a partner and share the actions you have come up with to manage the chronic procrastination problem. Indicate why you have starred certain actions. Allow your partner to ask questions to clarify what you are saying.
4. Reverse the process and have your partner do the same thing.
5. Change partners and deal with the delayed-project problem in the same way.
6. At home reflect on what you have learned about yourself in terms of action orientation and the need for action in managing problems and developing opportunities.

Example

Here are some of the action possibilities that Dahlia includes in her chronic-procrastination list:

10

* Reserve a half hour every day for the correspondence.
* Develop a sorting system. Throw away the junk immediately.
* Every day separate key letters from the rest. Do those immediately.
* Do the correspondence <u>with</u> my husband.
* Do other business tasks instead of the correspondence.
* Work a trade-off system. One month he does it, the next I do it.
* Get a third party to do the correspondence.
* Use the telephone and get others to use the telephone more, that is, cut down on the correspondence.
* Get a fax machine.
* Find ways of cutting down on the amount of correspondence we receive, for instance, get our names off mailing lists.

She then moves to the thornier delayed-project problem. Here are some of the items on her action list.

* Sit down with Kate and have longer-term planning meeting.
* Have her get her two other children involved.
* Tell her that I want to help her, not take her place.
* Do a bit of brainstorming as to who, besides the children, should get into this act.
* Help her find out what local governmental agencies have to offer.
* Talk to parents who have managed a similar problem.
* Find out if there are self-help groups for problems like this.
* See what private agencies have to offer.
* Talk to Kate about her feelings in all this. After all, I want to become a counselor. And I'm a kind of natural counselor anyway.
* Talk to Kate's kids before any kind of strategy meeting. Feel them out on this first.

After completing both lists, Dahlia goes back and puts a star in front of each item that has special potential.

The Learning Journal

Here are a few of the items in Dahlia's journal:

* I had no idea how often I talk about doing things without actually doing them. I could not possibly do all the things that I talk about doing. There is not enough time in the day. Therefore, I should start thinking of what my priorities are. When I say that I want to do something, I now want to ask myself, "In what category do you put that? Is it high, medium, or low priority?"
* I have never done this kind of brainstorming exercise before. I've learned that I have let my imagination grow stale.
* I've always seen myself as a "woman of action." I guess I am, compared to some. I do a lot of things, but not always the right things. I need more planning and focus in my life.

PART THREE

BASIC
COMMUNICATION
SKILLS

There are two sets of communication skills that are essential for helpers. The first set includes attending, listening, basic empathy, and probing and is the focus of the exercises in Part Three. The second set, communication skills associated with challenging clients, is dealt with in the exercises associated with Step I-B of the helping model--challenging clients' blind spots and helping them develop new, action-oriented perspectives.

I. EXERCISES IN ATTENDING

Your posture, gestures, facial expressions, and voice all send nonverbal messages to your clients. The purpose of the exercises in this section is to make you aware of the different kinds of nonverbal messages you send to clients and how to use nonverbal behavior to communicate with them. It is important that what you say verbally is reinforced rather than muddled or contradicted by your nonverbal messages.

Before doing these exercises, review the material on attending. Recall especially the basic elements of physical attending summarized by the acronym **SOLER**:

S Face your clients **SQUARELY**. This says that you are available to work with them.
O Adopt an **OPEN** posture. This says that you are open to your clients and want to be nondefensive.
L **LEAN** toward the client at times. This underscores your attentiveness and lets clients know that you are with them.
E Maintain good **EYE** contact without staring. This tells your clients of your interest in them and their concerns.
R Remain relatively **RELAXED** with clients as you interact with them. This indicates your confidence in what you are doing and also helps clients relax.

Of course, these are guidelines rather than hard and fast rules. There are two points. First, use your posture, gestures, facial expressions, and voice to send messages you want to clients, such as, "I want to work with you to help you manage your life better." Second, attend carefully so that you can **listen** carefully to clients.

EXERCISE 5: INITIAL SELF-ASSESSMENT OF ATTENDING BEHAVIORS

This is an exercise you do outside the training group in your everyday life. Observe your attending behaviors for a week--at home, with friends, at school, at work. You are not being asked to become preoccupied with the micro-behaviors of attending. Observe yourself enough to present a self-assessment to your fellow trainees in a week's time. Of course, even being asked to "watch yourself" will induce changes in your behavior; you will probably use more of the SOLER behaviors than you ordinarily do. The purpose of this exercise is to sensitize you to attending behaviors in general and to get some idea of what your day-to-day attending style looks like. First, read about attending skills in the text.

1. Catch yourself attending (or not attending) to others in the various social settings of your life.
2. Jot down the findings of your investigation.
3. Include what you do well and what needs improvement.
4. Share your assessment in the training group through whatever format your instructor determines.
5. As you listen to your co-learners, what themes emerge in terms of both the strengths and weaknesses of attending behavior in everyday life.

Don't read too little or too much into nonverbal behavior. In the training sessions, make sure that your nonverbal behavior is helping you work effectively with others and send the messages you want to send. Throughout the training program, observe the nonverbal behavior of your fellow trainees and give them feedback on how it affects you when you play the role of client or observer. Throughout the training program, ask for feedback on your own attending style.

EXERCISE 6: OBSERVING AND GIVING FEEDBACK ON QUALITY OF PRESENCE

More important than nonverbal behavior in itself is the total quality of your being with and working with your clients. Your posture and nonverbal behavior are a part of your presence, but there is more to presence than SOLER activities.

This is an exercise that pertains to the entire length of the training program. You are asked to give ongoing feedback both to yourself and to the other members of the training group on the quality of your presence to one another as you interact, learn, and practice helping skills. Here is a checklist to help you provide that feedback to your fellow helpers.

* How effectively is the helper using postural cues to indicate a willingness to work with the client?
* In what ways does the helper distract clients and observers from the task at hand, for instance, by fidgeting?
* How flexible is the helper is engaging in SOLER behaviors? To what degree do these behaviors help the counselor be with the client effectively?
* How natural is the helper in attending to the client? Are there any indications that the helper is not being himself or herself?
* From a physical point of view, what does the helper need to do to become more effectively present to his or her clients?

Since quality of presence involves both internal attitudes and external behaviors, trainees should not become preoccupied with the micro-skills of attending. However, they should take time, especially early on, to give one another feedback on attending behaviors. Since giving feedback is such an important part of any training program, the next section offers some guidelines on giving feedback effectively.

II. GIVING FEEDBACK

Giving feedback well is an art. Here are some guidelines to help you develop that art.

1. **Keep the goal of feedback in mind.** In giving feedback, always keep the generic goal of feedback in mind: To help the other person (or yourself, in the case of self-feedback) do a better job. Improved performance is the goal. Applied to helping, this means providing the kind of feedback to yourself and your co-learners that will help you become better helpers. Feedback will help you learn every stage and step of the model.

2. **Give positive feedback.** Tell your co-learners what they are doing well. This reinforces useful helping behaviors. "You leaned toward him and kept good eye contact even though he became very intense and emotional. Your behavior said, 'I'm still with you.'"

3. **Don't avoid corrective feedback.** To learn from our mistakes we must know what they are. Corrective feedback given in a humane way is a powerful tool for learning. "You seem reluctant to challenge your clients. For instance, Sam [the client] didn't fulfill his contract from the last meeting and you let it go. You fidgeted when he said he didn't get around to it."

4. **Be specific.** General statements like, "I liked your style in challenging your client," or "You could have been more understanding," are not helpful. Change them to statements such as, "Your challenge was helpful because you pointed out how self-defeating her internal conversations with herself are and hinted at ways she could change these conversations." or, "Your tone was harsh and you did not give him a chance to reply to what you were saying."

5. **Focus on behavior rather than traits.** Point out what the helper does or fails to do. Do not focus on traits or use labels such as, "You showed yourself to be a leader." or "You're still a bumbler." Avoid using negative traits such as "lazy," "a slow learner," "incompetent," "manipulative," and so forth. This is just namecalling and creates a negative learning climate in the group. The following statements deal with specific behaviors rather than traits. "You let him criticize you without becoming defensive; he listened to you better after that." or "You did not catch her core message; in fact, you seem to have difficulty in listening well enough to catch your clients' core messages." Such statements deal with specific behaviors rather than traits.

6. **Indicate the impact of the behavior on the client.** Feedback should help counselors-to-be interact more productively with clients. It helps, then, to indicate the impact of the helper's behavior on the client. "You interrupted the client three times in the space of about two minutes. After the third time, she spoke less intensely and switched to safer topics. She seemed to wander around."

7. **Provide hints for better performance.** Often helpers, once they receive corrective feedback, know how to change their behavior. After all, they are learning how to help in the training program. Sometimes, however, if the helper agrees with the feedback but does not know how to change his or her behavior, suggestions or hints on how to improve performance are useful. These, too, should be specific and clear. "You are having trouble providing your clients with empathy because you allow them to talk too long. They have made so many points that you don't know which to respond to. Try 'interrupting' your clients gently so that you can respond to key messages as they come up."

8. **Be brief.** Feedback that is both specific and brief is most helpful. Long-winded feedback proves to be a waste of time. A helper might need feedback on a number of points. In this case, provide feedback on one or two points. Give further feedback later on. In general, do not overload your co-learners with too much feedback at one time.

9. **Use dialogue.** Feedback is more effective if it takes place through a dialogue between the giver and receiver, a brief dialogue, of course. This gives the receiver an opportunity to clarify what the feedback giver means and to ask for suggestions if he or she needs them. A dialogue helps the receiver better "own" the feedback.

EXERCISE 7: GIVING FEEDBACK TO ONESELF

This exercise will enable you to get feedback on how well you provide feedback. In this case, you will be giving feedback to yourself.

1. Write down a helping-related area in which you could use some improvement.
2. Jot down one or two strengths in the area chosen and one or two things that need improvement.
3. In a small group, the size of which is to be determined by the instructor, give yourself feedback you have prepared. Each trainee takes a turn. After each is finished, he or she will receive feedback from the others on how well he or she lived up to the criteria for effective feedback outlined above.
4. Give the feedback in the second person, that is, speak to yourself as in the example below.

Example

John, a trainee, says:

"The helping-related area in which I am giving myself feedback is listening to others. Here's what I'd say to myself:

You listen well enough to capture other people's ideas. If asked, you could repeat them. And you don't discount others' ideas, at least not openly. However, you don't listen to learn anything new. Inside you're comparing what the other person is saying to what you think. Inside you're always asking, 'Is what this person is saying right or wrong? Does this agree with the way I think?' Then, when you respond, you come back with your own ideas and you push them hard. My best bet is that others feel discounted. They are hesitant to share with you what they really think. Try an experiment. Listen to others with the sole purpose of understanding what they have to say. Then find a way of letting them know that you understand what they've said without either agreeing or disagreeing with it.

Well, I could go on with a lot more but that's the basic idea."

5. Start this exercise by giving feedback to "John" on his feedback to himself. Briefly discuss what he did well and what he might improve. To what degree do you think John's feedback to himself will help him improve. Then do steps 1-4.

III. EXERCISES IN ACTIVE LISTENING

Effective helpers are active listeners. When you listen to clients, you listen to them discussing:

* their **experiences**, what they see as happening to them;
* their **behaviors**, what they do or fail to do;
* their **affect**, the feelings and emotions that arise from their experiences and behaviors; and
* their **points of view** in talking about their experiences, behaviors, and feelings.

Experiences, behaviors, and feelings can be either overt (capable of being seen by others) or covert (not seen by others, hidden "inside" the speaker).

*   **Overt experience:**   "He yelled at me."
*   **Covert experience:**   "Thoughts about death come out of nowhere and flood my mind."

*   **Overt behavior:**   "I spend about three hours every night in some bar."
*   **Covert behavior:**   "Before she comes over I plan everything I'm going to say."

*   **Overt emotion** (expressed):   "I got very angry and shouted at her."
*   **Covert emotion:**   (felt, but not expressed):   "I was delighted that he failed, but I didn't let on."

You can learn a great deal about clients by listening to their manners of speaking, that is, the mix of experiences, behaviors, and feelings they discuss and how specific or vague they are.

EXERCISE 8:   LISTENING TO YOUR OWN FEELINGS AND EMOTIONS

If you are to listen to the feelings and emotions of clients, you first should be familiar with your own emotional states.   A number of emotional states are listed below.   You are asked to describe what you feel when you feel these emotions.   Describe what you feel as <u>concretely</u> as possible: How does your body react? What happens inside you? What do you feel like doing? Consider the following examples.

Example 1

Accepted: When I feel accepted,

> I feel warm inside.
> I feel safe.
> I feel free to be myself.
> I feel like sitting back and relaxing.
> I feel I can let my guard down.
> I feel like sharing myself.
> I feel some of my fears easing away.
> I feel at home.
> I feel at peace.
> I feel my loneliness drifting away.

Example 2

Scared: When I feel very scared,

> my mouth dries up.
> my bowels become loose.
> there are butterflies in my stomach.
> I feel like running away.
> I feel very uncomfortable.
> I feel the need to talk to someone.
> I turn in on myself.
> I feel useless.
> I'm unable to concentrate.
> I feel very vulnerable.
> I sometimes feel like crying.

In order to keep this from becoming just an intellectual exercise, try to picture yourself in situations in which you have actually experienced these emotions.   Then write down what you see in your imagination.   Don't do all of these.   Rather, try your hand at the emotions you have difficulty with. It's important to listen to yourself when you are experiencing emotions that are not easy for you to handle.

1. accepted	11. defensive	22. lonely	
2. affectionate	12. disappointed	23. loving	
3. afraid	13. free	24. rejected	*pick 5*
4. angry	14. frustrated	25. repulsed	
5. anxious	15. guilty	26. respect	
6. attracted	16. hopeful	27. sad	
7. bored	17. hurt	28. satisfied	
8. belonging, being "in community"	18. inferior	29. shy	
	19. intimate	30. superior	
9. competitive	20. jealous	31. suspicious	
10. confused	21. joyful	32. trusting	

Once you have described how you feel when you feel these emotions, you should have a wider repertory of words, phrases, and statements both to describe your own emotional states and to identify emotional states in others. Listening to your own emotions is a prelude to listening to the feelings and emotions of others.

LISTENING TO EXPERIENCES AND BEHAVIORS

Although the feelings and emotions of clients (not to mention your own) are extremely important, sometimes helpers concentrate too much, or rather too exclusively, on them. Feelings and emotions need to be understood, both by helpers and by clients, in the **context** of the experiences and behaviors that give rise to them. On the other hand, when clients hide their feelings, both from themselves and from others, then it is necessary to listen carefully to cues indicating the existence of suppressed, ignored, or unmanaged emotion.

EXERCISE 9: LISTENING TO KEY EXPERIENCES, BEHAVIORS, AND EMOTIONS

Since feelings and emotions do not exist in a vacuum, in this exercise you are asked to "listen to" the kinds of experiences and behaviors that give rise to the client's feelings.

1. Read the following statements.
2. Jot down key experiences.
3. Jot down key behaviors.
4. Jot down feeling and emotions generated by the experiences and behaviors.

Example

A twenty-seven-year-old man is talking to a minister about a visit with his mother the previous day. "I just don't know what got into me! She kept nagging me the way she always does, asking me why I don't visit her more often. As she went on, I got more and more angry. (He looks away from the counselor down toward the floor.) I finally began screaming at her. I told her to get off my case. (He puts his hands over his face.) I can't believe what I did! I called her a bitch. (Shaking his head.) I called her a bitch about ten times and then I left and slammed the door in her face."

a. **Key experiences.** Mother's nagging.

b. **Key behaviors.** <u>Losing his temper with his mother, yelling at her, calling her name.</u>

_____

c. **Feelings/emotions generated.** <u>embarrassed, guilty, ashamed, distraught, extremely</u>

<u>disappointed with himself, remorseful.</u>_____

Note carefully: This man is talking **about** his anger but, at the moment, he is feeling and expressing the emotions listed above. Now try your hand at the following cases.

1. A woman, 40, married, no children: "These counseling sessions have really done me a great deal of good! I enjoy my work more. I actually look forward to meeting new people. My husband and I are talking more seriously and decently to each other. At times he's even tender toward me the way he used to be. There's just so much more freedom in my life!"

a. **Client's key experiences.** _____

_____

_____

b. **Client's key behaviors.** _____

_____

c. **Feelings/emotions generated.** _____

_____

2. A woman, 53, about to get divorced: "My husband and I just decided to get a divorce. (Her voice is very soft, her speech is slow, halting.) I really don't look forward to the legal part of it (pause) to <u>any</u> part of it to tell the truth. For the first time in my life I just sit around and think a lot. Or stare into space. I just don't know what to expect. (She sighs heavily.) I'm well into middle age. I don't think another marriage is possible. I just don't know what to expect."

a. **Client's key experiences.** _____

_____

b. **Client's key behaviors.** _____

_____

c. **Feelings/emotions generated.** _____

_____

3. A man, 45, with a daughter, 14, who was just hit by a car: "I should never have allowed my daughter to go to the movies alone. (He keeps wringing his hands.) I don't know what my wife will say when she gets home from work. (He grimaces.) She says I'm careless . . . but being careless with the kids . . . that's something else! (He stands up and walks around.) I almost feel as if I had broken Karen's arm, not the guy in that car. (He sits down, stares at the floor, keeps tapping his fingers on the desk.) I don't know."

a. Client's key experiences. _____

_____

b. Client's key behaviors. _____

_____

c. Feelings/emotions generated. _____

_____

4. A woman, 38, unmarried, talking about losing a friend: "My best friend has just turned her back on me. And I don't even know why! (said with great emphasis) From the way she acted, I think she has the idea that I've been talking behind her back. I simply have not! (also said with great emphasis) Damn! This neighborhood is <u>full</u> of spiteful gossips. She should know that. If she's been listening to those foulmouths who just want to stir up trouble. . . . She could at least tell me what's going on."

a. Client's key experiences. _____

_____

b. Client's key behaviors. _____

_____

c. Feelings/emotions generated. _____

_____

5. A senior in high school, 17, talking to his girl friend: "My teacher told me today that I've done better work than she ever expected. I always thought I could be good at my studies if I applied myself. (He smiles.) So I tried this semester and it's paid off. It's really paid off!"

a. Client's key experiences. _____

_____

b. Client's key behaviors. _____

_____

c. Feelings/emotions generated. _____

_____

6. A trainee, 29, speaking to the members of his training group: "I don't know what to expect in this group. (He speaks hesitatingly.) I've never been in this kind of group before. From what I've seen so far, I, well, I get the feeling that you're pros, and I keep watching myself to see if I'm doing things right. (Sighs heavily.) I'm comparing myself to what everyone else is doing. I want to get good at this stuff . . . (pause) . . . but frankly I'm not sure I can make it."

a. **Client's key experiences.** _____

_____

b. **Client's key behaviors.** _____

_____

c. **Feelings/emotions generated.** _____

_____

7. A young women, 20, speaking to a college counselor toward the end of her second year: "I've been in college almost two years now, and nothing much has happened. (She speaks listlessly.) The teachers here are only so-so. I thought they'd be a lot better. At least that's what I heard. And I can't say much for the social life here. Things go on the same from day to day, from week to week."

a. **Client's key experiences.** _____

_____

b. **Client's key behaviors.** _____

_____

c. **Feelings/emotions generated.** _____

_____

8. A man, 64, who has been told that he has terminal cancer, speaking to a medical resident: "Why me? Why me? I'm not even that old! And I don't smoke or anything like that. (He begins to cry.) Look at me. I thought I had some guts. I'm just a slobbering mess. Oh God, why terminal? What are these next months going to be like? (Pause, he stops crying.) What would you care! I'm just a failure to you guys."

a. **Client's key experiences.** _____

_____

b. **Client's key behaviors.** _____

_____

c. **Feelings/emotions generated.** _____

_____

9. A woman, 42, married, with three children in their early teens, speaking to a church counselor: "Why does my husband keep blaming me for his trouble with the kids? I'm always in the middle. He complains to me about them. They complain to me about him. (She looks the counselor straight in the eye and talks very deliberately.) I could walk out on the whole thing right now. Who the hell do they think they are?"

a. **Client's key experiences.** _____

b. **Client's key behaviors.** _____

_____

c. **Feelings/emotions generated.** _____

_____

10. A bachelor, 39, speaking to the members of a life-style group to which he has belonged for about a year: "I've finally met a woman who is very genuine and who lets me be myself. I can care deeply about her without making a child out of her. (He is speaking in a soft, steady voice.) And she cares about me without mothering me. I never thought it would happen. (He raises his voice a bit.) Is it actually happening to me? Is it actually happening?"

a. **Client's key experiences.** _____

_____

b. **Client's key behaviors.** _____

_____

c. **Feelings/emotions generated.** _____

_____

11. A girl in her late teens who is serving a two-year term in a reformatory speaks to a probation counselor: (She sits silently for a while and doesn't answer any question the counselor puts to her. Then she shakes her head and looks around the room.) "I don't know what I'm doing here. You're the third counselor they've sent me to . . . or is it the fourth? It's a waste of time! Why do they keep making me come here? (She looks straight at the counselor.) Let's fold the show right now. You're not getting anything out of me. Come on, get smart."

a. **Client's key experiences.** _____

_____

b. **Client's key behaviors.** _____

_____

c. **Feelings/emotions generated.** _____

_____

12. A man, 54, talking to a counselor about a situation at work: "I don't know where to turn. They're asking me to do things at work that I just don't think are right. If I don't do them, well, I'll probably be let go. And I don't know where I'm going to get another job at my age in this economy. But if I do what they want me to, I think I could get into trouble, I mean legal trouble. I'd be the fall guy. My head's spinning. I've never had to face anything like this before. Where do I turn?"

a. **Client's key experiences.** _____

_____

b. **Client's key behaviors.** _____

_____

c. **Feelings/emotions generated.** _____

_____

EXERCISE 10: RELATING LISTENING TO ACTION

In this exercise you are asked to identify not only feelings and emotions and the key or relevant experiences and behaviors that give rise to them, but also actions that the client might take to manage his or her problem situation better. It is not that you are going to tell the client what to do. But helping clients adopt an action orientation to their problem situations is central to helping. This exercise will help you develop that orientation in yourself.

1. Identify key feelings.
2. Identify key experiences and behaviors.
3. List some common-sense actions you might consider taking in order to manage the problem situation, if you were the client.

Example

A seventh-grade boy talking to a teacher he trusts (all this is said in a halting voice and he does not look at the teacher): "Something happened yesterday that's bothering me a lot. I was looking out the window after school. It was late. I saw two of the guys, the bullies, beating up on one of my best friends. I was afraid to go down. . . . A coward. . . . I didn't tell anyone, I didn't do anything."

Feelings. _ashamed, guilty, down, miserable_ _____

Relevant experience. _watching a good friend get beat up_ _____

Relevant behavior. _failing to help his friend_ _____

Possible client actions. _Just getting it off his chest as he is now;_ _____

talking with his friend; apologizing; finding out how he wants to handle similar situations in

the future _____

In this case the client's behavior, <u>not helping</u>, seems to be key to how he is feeling as he talks with the teacher. There are a number of things he might do to help himself manage his current misery.

1. A young woman talking to a counselor in a center for battered women: "This is the third time he's beaten me up. I didn't come before because I still can't believe it! We're married only a year. After we got married, he began ordering me around in ways he never did before we got married. He'd get furious if I questioned him. Then he began shoving me if I didn't

do what he wanted fast or right. And I just let him do it! I just let him do it! (She breaks down and sobs.) And now three beatings in about four weeks. Oh God, what's happened?"

Feelings. _____

Relevant experience. _____

_____

Relevant behavior. _____

_____

Possible client actions. _____

_____

2. A girl, 12, talking to a psychologist at a time when her parents are involved in a divorce case: "I still want to do something to help, but I can't. I just can't! They won't let me. When they would fight and get real mean and were screaming at each other, I'd run and try to get in between them. One or the other would push me away. They wouldn't pay any attention to me at all. They're still pushing me away. They don't care how I think or feel or what happens to me! My mother tells me that kids should stay out of things like this."

Feelings. _____

Relevant experience. _____

_____

Relevant behavior. _____

_____

Possible client actions. _____

_____

3. A man, 25, in a counselor training group talking to the trainer: "I've been sitting here watching you give Peggy feedback. You're doing it very well. But I'm also saying to myself, 'Why isn't he that helpful and that careful with me?' I want the same kind of feedback, but you don't say much to me at all. I'm as active as anyone else in the group. I volunteer to act as both counselor and client. I don't know why you pass me by. Is all of this just my imagination?"

Feelings. _____

Relevant experience. _____

_____

Relevant behavior. _____

_____

Possible client actions. _____

_____

4. A woman, 35, with two children, one four, one six, whose husband has deserted them, is talking to a social worker: "He's not sending me any money. I don't even know where he is. They're asking me for the rent and telling me that I'll be out if I don't come up with it. I've been to two different agencies and filled out all sorts of forms, but I don't have any money or food stamps yet. I've been getting food from my mother, but she's really got next to nothing. What am I supposed to do? I'll work, but who's to take care of the kids. I asked all around and there's no day-care center anywhere near here."

Feelings. _____

Relevant experience. _____

_____

Relevant behavior. _____

_____

Possible client actions. _____

_____

5. A man, 53, is talking to a counselor a few months after the sudden death of his wife. His two children are married and living in distant towns. "I miss her so. The house seems so empty. At my job I work alone on computer programming. There's no one I talk to at work. Now there's no one at home. I walk around the house thinking of how I was with her in each room. At night sometimes I sit in the dark thinking of nothing. We had few friends, so no one calls. And I haven't seen either of the kids since the funeral."

Feelings. _____

Relevant experience. _____

_____

Relevant behavior. _____

_____

Possible client actions. _____

_____

6. A woman, 63, in a hospital dying of cancer, is talking to a member of the pastoral counseling staff: "I can understand it from my children, but not from my husband. I know I'm dying. But he comes here with a brave smile every day, hiding what he feels. We never talk about my dying. I know he's trying to protect me, but it's so unreal. I don't tell him that his constant cheerfulness and his refusal to talk about my sickness are actually painful to me. (She shakes her head.) I'm being careful of <u>him</u>!"

Feelings. _____

Relevant experience. _____

_____

Relevant behavior. _____

_____

Possible client actions. _____

_____

7. A freshman in college talking to a counselor toward the end of his first year: "One week I find myself studying hard, working on the school paper, going to a talk on foreign affairs. The next week I'm boozing it up, looking around for a hot sex partner, and playing cards all day with the boys. It's like being two different people who don't even know each other! I like being in college, away from home and all that. But when I'm here I don't know what I want."

Feelings. _____

Relevant experience. _____

_____

Relevant behavior. _____

_____

Possible client actions. _____

_____

8. A man, 70, arrested for stealing funds from the company where he has worked for 25 years, talking to his lawyer: "To tell you the truth, it's probably a good thing I've been caught. I've been stealing on and off for the last five or six years. It's been a game. It soaked up my energies, my attention, distracted me from thinking about getting old. Now I'm saying to myself: 'You old fool, what're you running from?' I've been forcing myself to try to make sense out of my life. You're probably thinking: 'It's about time, old guy.' I'm thinking it's as good a time as any."

Feelings. _____

Relevant experience. _____

_____

Relevant behavior. _____

_____

Possible client actions. _____

_____

9. A woman, 37, married, with an unwanted pregnancy; she has two children, one in the seventh and one in the eighth grade; she is talking to another woman, her closest friend:

"Ellen, I just don't know what to do. I've talked to my pastor, but I knew what he was going to say. He wasn't much help at all. Oh, God, I don't want another child! Not now! A couple of people I know just assume I'll have an abortion. That's what they'd do. I won't have an abortion, I just won't. But I don't want to have to restructure my life. I've had the children I wanted!"

Feelings. _____

Relevant experience. _____

_____

Relevant behavior. _____

_____

Possible client actions. _____

_____

10. A boy, 11, who has been sexually abused by an older male relative, talking to a counselor (he speaks in a hesitant, agitated voice): "I liked him a lot. He was always nice to me. He took me to ball games. He gave me spending money. I mean he was not some kind of jerk. He was really kind. He was drunk when it happened. I trusted him. I wasn't even sure what was happening. I don't know what to think. Maybe I shouldn't have said anything. He looked so awful when I saw him yesterday. I <u>had</u> to say something, didn't I?"

Feelings. _____

Relevant experience. _____

_____

Relevant behavior. _____

_____

Possible client actions. _____

_____

11. A minister who has been having an affair with one of his parishioners, talking to another minister: "I've never known anyone like her before. It was as if it didn't make any difference that both of us were married. I've never experienced such strong emotion. I can tell myself exactly what I should do. But I don't do it. We avoid talking about where all this is going to lead. I know in the back of my mind that my family and career and all that are on the line, but I keep it pushed back. There's doom on the horizon, but the present is so damn full!"

Feelings. _____

Relevant experience. _____

_____

Relevant behavior. _____

_____

Possible client actions. _____

_____

EXERCISE 11: LISTENING TO THE CLIENT'S POINT OF VIEW

Empathic listening is listening to and understanding the client's point of view in terms of experiences, behaviors, and feelings. Even when you think the client's point of view needs to be challenged, it is essential to hear it. The following instructions apply to both A and B below.

1.   Read the paragraph. Try to picture the clients saying what they say. Listen carefully.
2.   Go over the paragraph sentence by sentence. Identify experiences, behaviors, and feelings.
3.   Summarize the client's point of view in terms of key experiences, key behaviors, and key feelings/emotions. Do not evaluate it or contaminate it with your own point of view.

A. The following client is a 40-year-old woman who has just lost her job. She is talking about the events before, during, and after her being fired.

"Yesterday I was talking with one of the punch-press operators when my boss storms in and begins raking me over the coals for a work stoppage I had nothing to do with. I stood there in shock. I was so angry that I wanted to yell back at him, but I kept my cool. But all day I couldn't get it out of my mind. No matter what I was doing, it haunted me. I finally got so angry that I burst into his office and told him just what I thought of him. I even let him have it for a few lousy things he's done in the past. He fired me on the spot. Last night I was pretty depressed. And all day today I've been trying to figure out where I can get a new job or maybe how I can get my old job back."

What is this client's point of view? _____

_____

_____

_____

_____

B. This client is a 37-year-old man who is talking to a counselor for the first time. He has been referred by a doctor who has find no physical basis for a variety of somatic complaints.

"My wife keeps putting me down.   For instance, last week she got a job without even discussing it with me. She didn't even ask me how I'd feel. She doesn't share what's going on inside. She makes big decisions without letting me in on the process. I'm sure she sees me as weak and ineffectual. She's just like her mother. My mother-in-law never wanted me to marry her. She was too good for me. Now my wife does everything to prove that her mother is right. She would never admit it, of course, but that's the way she is. I wouldn't be surprised that her goal is to earn more money than I do. I see other guys getting divorces for a lot less than I have to put up with. But that would make both of them happy. I asked her to come with me to see you and she laughed at me, she actually laughed at me."

27

What is this client's point of view? _____

_____

_____

_____

_____

_____

In a small group, compare your summaries of these clients' points of view with those of your fellow trainees. What did you learn from this discussion?

Finally, in the total training group discuss whether some aspects of the client's point of view might, eventually, need to be challenged.

IV. COMMUNICATING UNDERSTANDING: EXERCISES IN BASIC EMPATHY

Basic empathy is the communication to another person of your understanding of his or her point of view with respect to his or her experiences, behaviors, and feelings. It is a skill you need throughout the helping model. Focusing on the client's point of view without necessarily agreeing with it is very useful in establishing and developing relationships with clients and in helping them clarify both problem situations and unexploited opportunities, in setting goals, and in developing strategies and plans. The starting point of the entire helping process and each of its steps is the client's point of view, even when it needs to be challenged.

The exercises in the previous section emphasized your ability to listen to and understand the client's point of view. The exercises in this section relate to your ability to **communicate** this understanding to the client.

Empathy focuses on the client's key messages--key experiences, key behaviors, key feelings and emotions, and key decisions. Sometimes experiences take front and center, sometimes behaviors, sometimes emotions, sometimes decisions. Therefore, the "formula" for basic empathy can take two forms:

Form 1

"You feel . . ." (followed by the right emotion and some indication of its intensity) "because . . ." (followed by the key experiences and/or behaviors that give rise to the emotion). For example:

* "You feel great because you did much better in the exams than you had ever hoped."
* "You feel annoyed with yourself because you don't say anything or do anything about the way she mistreats you."

Form 2

This simply reverses the order: "Because . . . (followed by key experiences and/or behaviors) "you feel . . ." (followed by the correct emotion and the right intensity. For example:

* "Because she left town without calling you, you feel a bit hurt.
* "Because he put his pride aside and asked you directly for help and you didn't even answer him, you feel guilty."

To a degree, Form 1 emphasizes feelings and emotions, while Form 2 emphasizes experiences and behaviors. Remember, however, that managing emotions usually means managing the experiences and actions that give rise to them. The importance of emotions should not be underemphasized,
but it should not be overemphasized either. In many of your interchanges with clients, feelings and emotions will not be a key factor. For instance, Tom is discussing some goals that might help him manage his passivity.

Tom: I'm not sure where to begin. I hardly ever say anything at the dorm meetings, even though I often have strong opinions on the issues being discussed. One general goal would be to speak up at these meetings. I mean make it a rule to speak to any issue I have some interest in.

Helper: So a pattern of speaking up rather than just listening would be one way to start managing what've you've described as being "just a bit too passive."

The helper communicates understanding of one of Tom's possible goals, but feelings and emotions do not play a significant role.

EXERCISE 12: COMMUNICATING UNDERSTANDING OF A CLIENT'S FEELINGS

When feelings and emotions do constitute a part of client's core message, an understanding of them needs to be communicated to him or her. Clients express feelings and helpers can communicate an understanding of feelings in a variety of ways:

* **By single words:**

    I feel good.
    I'm depressed.
    I feel abandoned.
    I'm delighted.
    I feel trapped.
    I'm angry.

* **By different kinds of phrases:**

    I'm sitting on top of the world.
    I feel down in the dumps.
    I feel left in the lurch.
    I feel tip top.
    My back's up against the wall.
    I'm really steaming.

* **By what is implied in a behavioral statements** (what action I feel like taking):

    I feel like giving up. (implied emotion: despair)
    I feel like hugging you. (implied emotion: joy)
    I feel like smashing him in the face. (implied emotion: severe anger)
    Now that it's over, I feel like dancing in the streets. (implied emotions: relief and joy)

* **By what is implied in experiences that are revealed:**

    I feel I'm being dumped on. (implied feeling: anger)

29

I feel I'm being stereotyped. (implied feeling: resentment)
I feel I'm at the top of her list. (implied feeling: joy)
I feel I'm going to catch my lunch. (implied feeling: apprehension)

Note here that the implication could be spelled out:

I feel angry because I'm being dumped on.
I resent the fact that I'm being stereotyped.
I feel great because I believe I'm at the top of her list.
I'm apprehensive because I think I'm going to catch my lunch.

1. A number of situations involving different kinds of feelings and emotions are listed below. Picture yourself talking to this person.
2. Use two of the four ways of communicating understanding of the client's feelings listed below.

Example

Sally tells you that she has just been given the kind of job she has been looking for for the past two years.

Single word: You're really happy.
A phrase: You're on cloud nine.
Experiential statement: You feel you got what you deserve.
Behavioral statement: You feel like going out and celebrating.

Now express the following feelings and emotions in two different ways (single word, phrase, experiential statement, and/or behavioral statement).

1. This woman is about to go to her daughter's graduation from college. She never thought that her daughter would make it through. She has invested a lot of money and a lot of emotion in her daughter's education. Now the day has arrived.

a. _____

_____

b. _____

_____

2. This women has just had her purse stolen. She had just cashed her bi-weekly paycheck and the money was in the purse. She has had a streak of bad luck. Her sister was in an auto accident. Her only son was detained by the police for a minor theft. There has not been much good news at all.

a. _____

_____

b. _____

_____

3. This man is waiting for the results of medical tests. He has been losing weight for about two months and has been feeling tired and listless all the time. He is the kind of person who does not like to face up to bad news. That's why he kept putting off the tests. He ends by

saying, "I . . . well, I just don't know where I stand. Nobody said anything to me during the tests."

a. _____

_____

b. _____

_____

4. A prospective employer has just found out that this client has a criminal record. The client had hoped that he would get the job and prove himself before anyone found out about his record. He has just received a call telling him that he is no longer being considered for the job. Nevertheless, he says, "Well, I did what I thought was right. I never had the intention of deceiving anyone. I'm going to make it, somehow."

a. _____

_____

b. _____

_____

5. This woman has just lost a custody case for her children. She never dreamed that the court would award custody to her husband whom she sees as selfish and spiteful. During the interview she seems almost in a daze. She ends by saying, "It's all over now."

a. _____

_____

b. _____

_____

6. This young man has just been abandoned by his wife. They have been married for about a year. She left a note saying, "This has not been working out." He thought that things were going fairly well. He goes into a long description of what he's going to do to get her back. He ends by asking in a somewhat pleading voice, "Can you make someone love you?"

a. _____

_____

b. _____

_____

7. Bruno's boss has just told him that the project he has been working on is succeeding far beyond his expectations. He told him that he has probably been underestimating him all along and is thinking of using him in a more critical job. This is all news to Bruno who has been relatively content at work. He does not know what to think about what his boss has told him. He feels a fair amount of ambiguity about being singled out like this.

a. _____

_____

b. _____

_____

8. This woman has been suffering from migraine headaches for a long time. They seem to be getting worse. So far nothing has helped her to reduce their number or to manage them once they start. She won't go to a doctor and has refused to read anything about newer treatments for this kind of headache. "It's the same old stuff," she says, "promising you a lot and delivering nothing."

a. _____

_____

b. _____

_____

9. This woman has been told that there might be a cure for her child's life-threatening illness. She is also told that the cure is experimental and might not work. The woman says, "It's got to work!"

a. _____

_____

b. _____

_____

10. This man is talking about having to work two jobs to support his family. He's fortunate to have both jobs, but he has no time for himself. The jobs eat into his evening hours and the weekends. His family does not seem to notice his absence. They take for granted all the hours he has been putting in. He ends by saying, "It's as if life is about nothing else but work."

a. _____

_____

b. _____

_____

EXERCISE 13: RELATING EMPATHY TO ACTION

In this exercise you are asked to do three things: (1) use the "you feel . . . because . . ." formula (or its reverse) to communicate empathy to the client; (2) recast your response in your own words while still identifying both feelings and the experiences and/or behaviors that underlie the feelings; and (3) indicate some possible actions the client could take, but not in an advice-giving mode.

Example

A married woman, 31, is talking to a counselor about her marriage: "I can't believe it! You know when Tom and I were here last week we made a contract that said that he would be home for supper every evening and on time. Well, he came home on time every day this past week. I never dreamed that he would live up to his part of the bargain so completely!"

Formula. "Because he really stuck to his word, you feel great!"

Non-formula. "He really surprised you by doing it right!"

Possible client actions. The client could let her husband know how pleased she is, make sure that she keeps her part of the bargain, stop telling herself that her marriage is impossible.

Now imagine yourself listening intently to each of the clients quoted below. First use the "You feel . . . because . . ." formula or its reverse; then use your own words. Try to make the second response sound as natural (as much like yourself) as possible. After you use your own words, check to see if you have both a "you feel" part and a "because" part in your response.

1. This man, 40, is talking about his invalid mother: "I know she's using her present illness to control me. How could a 'good' son refuse any of her requests at a time like this? (He pounds his fist on the arm of his chair.) But it's all part of a pattern. She's used one thing or another to control me all my life. If I let things go on like this, she'll make me feel responsible for her death!"

Formula. _____

_____

Your own words. _____

_____

Possible client actions. _____

_____

_____

2. A woman, 25, talking about her current boyfriend: "I can't quite figure him out. (She pauses, shakes her head slowly, and then speaks quite slowly.) I just can't figure out whether he really cares about me or if he's just trying to get me into bed. I've been burned before; I don't want to get burned again."

Formula. _____

_____

Your own words. _____

_____

Possible client actions. _____

_____

_____

3. A businessman, 38, talking to a close associate: "I really don't know what my boss wants. I don't know what he thinks of me. He tells me I'm doing fine even though I don't think that I'm doing anything special. Then he blows up over nothing at all. I keep asking myself if there's something wrong with me, I mean, that I don't see what's getting him to act the way he does. I'm beginning to wonder if this is the right job for me."

Formula. _____

_____

Your own words. _____

_____

Possible client actions. _____

_____

_____

4. A woman, 73, in the hospital with a broken hip: "When you get old, you have to expect things like this to happen. It could have been much worse. When I lie here, I keep thinking of the people in the world who are a lot worse off than I am. I'm not a complainer. Oh, I'm not saying that this is fun or that the people in this place give you the best service--who does these days?--but it's a good thing that these hospitals exist. Think of those who don't have anything."

Formula. _____

_____

Your own words. _____

_____

Possible client actions. _____

_____

_____

5. A seventh-grade girl to her teacher, outside class: "My classmates don't like me, and right now I don't like them! Why do they have to be so mean? They make fun of me--well, they make fun of my clothes. My family can't afford what some of those snots wear. Gee, they don't have to like me, but I wish they'd stop making fun of me."

Formula. _____

_____

Your own words. _____

_____

Possible client actions. _____

_____

_____

6. A high school counselor, 41, talking to a colleague: "Sometimes I think I'm living a lie. I don't have any interest in high school kids anymore. So when they come into my office, I don't really do much to help them. Most of them and their problems bore me. But I've been here now for twelve years. I like living around here. I try half-heartedly to work up some interest, but I don't get far."

Formula. _____

_____

Your own words. _____

_____

Possible client actions. _____

_____

_____

7. A man, 35, who has not been feeling well, talking to a friend who is a nurse: "I'm going into the hospital tomorrow for some tests. I think they suspect an ulcer. (He fidgets.) But nobody has told me exactly what kind of tests. I'm supposed to take these enemas and not eat anything after supper this evening. I've heard rumors about these kinds of tests, but I'm not really sure what they're like. I'm not even sure that I want to know."

Formula. _____

_____

Your own words. _____

_____

Possible client actions. _____

_____

_____

8. A graduate student, 25, to her advisor: "I have two term papers due tomorrow. I'm giving a report in class this afternoon. My husband is down with the flu. And now I find out that the student committee wants to 'talk' with me about my 'progress' in the program. I think the last straw must be around here someplace."

Formula. _____

_____

Your own words. _____

_____

Possible client actions. _____

_____

_____

9. A woman, 43, talking to a counselor in a rape crisis center: "It was all I could do to come here. A friend told me to call the police. I didn't. I didn't want to become one of those stories you read in the paper everyday! They'd be asking me all sorts of questions. And hinting that it was probably my fault. Ugh! I just want to forget it. I don't want to keep reliving it over and over again."

Formula. _____

_____

Your own words. _____

_____

Possible client actions. _____

_____

_____

10. A female high school student, 17, talking to a male counselor about an unexpected pregnancy: "I, well, I don't think I can talk about it here. (pause) You being a man and all that. (pause) What happens between me and my boyfriend and me and my family--well, that's all very personal. I don't talk to strangers about personal things."

Formula. _____

_____

Your own words. _____

_____

Possible client actions. _____

_____

_____

EXERCISE 14: EMPATHY AND ACTION WITH CLIENTS FACING DILEMMAS

Clients sometimes talk about conflicting values, experiences, behaviors, and emotions. Responding with empathy means communicating an understanding of the conflict. Consider the following example.

Example

A woman, 32, talking to a counselor about adopting a child: "I'm going back and forth, back and forth. I say to myself, 'I really want a child,' but then I think about Bill [her husband] and his reluctance. He so wants our child and is so reluctant to raise someone else's. We don't even know why we can't have children. Both of us have avoided seeing a specialist. Neither wants to be the one 'at fault.' At times when I so want to be a mother I think I should marry someone who would be willing to adopt a child. But I love Bill and don't want to point an accusing finger at him."

Identify the conflict or dilemma. She believes that she runs the risk of alienating her husband if she insists on adopting a child, even though she strongly favors adoption.

Formula. "You feel trapped between your desire to be a mother and your love for your husband."

Non-formula. "You're caught in the middle. Adopting a child would solve one problem but perhaps create another."

Client action possibilities. She could keep pushing her husband, give up the idea of adopting a child, see a specialist on her own, ask him to go with her to a specialist, have a "no-decision" brainstorming session with Bill to expand action possibilities.

1. A factory worker, 30: "Work is okay. I do make a good living, and both my family and I like the money. My wife and I are both from poor homes, and we're living much better than we did when we were growing up. But the work I do is the same thing day after day. I may not be the world's brightest person, but there's a lot more to me than I use on those machines."

The conflict. _____

Formula. _____

_____

_____

Your own words. _____

_____

_____

Action possibilities. _____

_____

_____

2. A mental hospital patient, 54, who has spent five years in the hospital; he is talking to the members of an ongoing therapy group. Some of the members have been asking him what he's doing to get out. They point out the tendency to "push people out." He says, "To tell the truth, I like it here. I'm safe and secure. So why are so many people here so damn eager to see me out? Is it a crime because I feel comfortable here? (Pause, then in a more conciliatory voice.) I know you're all interested in me. I see that you care. But do I have to please you by doing something I don't want to do?"

The conflict. _____

_____

Formula. _____

_____

_____

Your own words. _____

_____

_____

Action possibilities. _____

_____

3. A juvenile probation officer to a colleague: "These kids drive me up the wall. Sometimes I think I'm really stupid for doing this kind of work. They taunt me. They push me as far as they can. To some of them I'm just another 'pig.' But every time I think of quitting--and this gets me--I know I'd miss the work and even miss the kids one way or another. When I wake up in the morning, I know the day's going to be full and it's going to demand everything I've got."

The conflict. _____

_____

Formula. _____

_____

_____

Your own words. _____

_____

_____

Action possibilities. _____

_____

4. A high school teacher, 50, to the principal: "Cindy Smith really got to me today. She's been a thorn in my side all semester. Just a little bitch. Asking questions in her 'sweet' way, but everyone knows she's trying to make an ass of me. Little snot! So I let her have it--I let it all come out and pasted her up against the wall--verbally, that is. But, damn, that's just what she wanted! You know me; I just don't do that kind of thing. I lost control. It was a pretty bad mistake."

The conflict. _____

_____

Formula. _____

_____

_____

Your own words. _____

_____

_____

Action possibilities. _____

_____

_____

5. A widowed mother, 47, talking about her son, 18: "He knows he can take advantage of me. If he stops talking to me or acts sullen for a couple of days, I go crazy. He gets everything he wants out of me, and I know it's my own fault. But I still love him very much. After all, he stays here with me. I do have a man in the house. He's going to be going to college locally, so he'll be around for a good while yet."

The conflict. _____

_____

Formula. _____

_____

_____

Your own words. _____

_____

Action possibilities. _____

_____

_____

_____

EXERCISE 15: COMMUNICATING UNDERSTANDING OF ONE ANOTHER'S POINTS OF VIEW

Another person's point of view is made up of not only of experiences, behaviors, and feelings, but also the interpretation or the slant the person gives to these. Empathy, then, includes this slant, even though you think the slant needs to be challenged. Challenging a person's interpretations of his or her experiences, behaviors, and feelings may be necessary. This is dealt with in Step I-B of the helping model.

1.   Divide into groups of three. The roles in each group are speaker, listener, and observer.
2.   Take a few minutes to prepare a statement on an issue that you believe to be important. You may jot down a few notes, but the statement is to be spoken, not read. You should be able to deliver the statement in less than a minute.
3.   After determining who is to go first, the speaker delivers his or her statement to the listener, while the observer watches.
4.   The listener listens carefully and then summarizes the point of view for the speaker. The listener begins with the phrase: "This, I believe, is your point of view." Your communication of empathy should be relatively brief and deal with the other person's core message or messages.
5.   Using the criteria outlined in the section on feedback above, both the speaker and the observer give feedback to the listener on his or her conciseness and accuracy.
6.   The process continues until each member of the group has played all three roles.

Example

Janine is the first to take the speaker's role. She says:

"As you can tell, I have a speech defect. As you might not be able to tell, at least not immediately, I'm also fairly bright. Also, while I'm not a stunning beauty, I'm not that bad looking. But the first thing a lot of people latch on to is the speech problem. I have more than a sneaking suspicion that this colors their view of me. My looks and my intelligence are seen through the filter of my speech. Often enough, I get discounted. I'm not exactly blaming people for that. It's so easy to do. But it leaves me feeling defensive much of the time. And I find that very uncomfortable."

Bernice, in the listener's role, summarizes Janine's point of view like this:

"This, I believe, is your point of view. You're angry at people because they don't take you as you are. You'd like to tell them about yourself, but they don't want to listen. You have to defend yourself all the time, and that's annoying."

Carla, in the observer role, gives feedback to Bernice. If you were Carla, what would you say to Bernice? In what ways did she capture the speaker's point of view? In what ways did she fall short? What might she have said?

EXERCISE 16: THE PRACTICE OF EMPATHY IN EVERYDAY LIFE

If the communication of accurate empathy is to become a part of your natural communication style, you will have to practice it outside formal training sessions. That is, it must become part of your everyday communication style or it will tend to lack genuineness in helping situations. Practicing empathy "out there" is a relatively simple process.

1.   **Empathy as an improbable event.** Empathy is not a normative response in everyday conversations. Find this out for yourself. Observe everyday conversations. Count how many times empathy is used as a response in any given conversation.

2.   **Your own use of empathy.** Next try to observe how often you yourself use empathy as part of your normal style. In the beginning, don't try to increase the number of times you use empathy in day-to-day conversations. Merely observe your usual behavior. What part does empathy normally play in your style?

3.   **Increasing your empathic responses.** Begin to increase the number of times you use accurate empathy. Be as natural as possible. Do not overwhelm others with this response; rather try to incorporate it gradually into your style. You will probably discover that there are quite a few opportunities for using empathy without being phony. Keep some sort of record of how often you use empathy in any given conversation.

4.   **The impact of empathy.** Observe the impact your use of empathy has on others. Don't set our to use others for the purpose of experimentation but, as you gradually increase your use of this communication skill naturally, try to see how it influences your conversations. What impact does it have on you? What impact does it have on others?

5.   **Learnings.** In a forum set up by the instructor, discuss with your fellow trainees what you have learned from this "experiment."

If empathy becomes part of your communication style "out there," then you should appear more and more natural in using empathy in the training program, both in playing the role of the helper and in listening and providing feedback to your fellow trainees. On the other hand, if you use empathy only in the training sessions, it will most likely remain artificial.

V. EXERCISES IN THE USE OF PROBES

Review the material on probes before doing the exercises in this section. A probe is a statement or a question that invites a client to discuss an issue more fully. Probes are ways of getting at important details that clients do not think of or are reluctant to talk about. They can be used at any point in the helping process to clarify issues, search for missing data, expand perspectives, and point toward possible client actions. An overuse of probes can lead to gathering a great deal of irrelevant information. The purpose of a probe is not information for its own sake, but data that serves the process of problem management and opportunity development.

EXERCISE 17: PROBING FOR CLARITY OF EXPERIENCES, BEHAVIORS, AND FEELINGS

In this exercise, brief problem situations will be presented. Your job is to formulate two possible probes.

1. First respond with empathy.
2. Identify something you would like expanded or clarified.

3. Indicate why you are choosing that particular issue or area.
4. Formulate and use a probe with the client.

Example

A woman, 24, complains that she is severely tempted to be unfaithful to her husband. Although she has not had an extended affair, she has had a few sexual encounters and feels that some day she will pursue a longer relationship. She does not blame herself or him. She merely says that her feelings are so strong that he cannot satisfy her. She wants more affection than he can possibly give. She fears that no one man will do so. During the interview she says, "I don't know whether I'm just being selfish or whether I just need to experiment more with relationships."

Response #1

a. **Empathic statement.** Given the strength of your sexual and affectional needs, you feel that now is the time to learn what part they are to play in your life.

b. **Issue to be explored more fully.** What she thinks about the issue of "selfishness," which she herself brings up.

c. **Why this issue?** Since all closer relationships involve give and take, her views on mutuality need to be clarified.

d. **Possible probe.** "I'm curious what you say to yourself when you 'talk' to yourself about possibly being 'selfish.'"

Response #2

a. **Empathic statement.** There is an urgency to do something and some kind of experimentation seems to make sense.

b. **Issue to be explored more fully.** The purpose of the "experimenting" she is talking about.

c. **Why this issue?** The whole concept of "experimenting more with relationships" is not clear nor what it might achieve.

d. **Possible probe.** "Let's focus on the 'experimenting.' What might that look like and how might it help you manage things better?"

Note that the first probe is a statement while the second is an open-ended question. Use a variety of probes--requests, statements, questions. Avoid an overuse of questions. When the probe is a question, make sure that it is open-ended.

1. Grace, 19, an unmarried, first-year college student, comes to counseling because of an unexpected and unwanted pregnancy. At present, she knows that the father could be either of

two young men. She is not sure what she wants to do about the baby. She has not yet told her parents, but thinks that they will be sympathetic. This is your third interview with Grace. She says, "I've gotten myself into this mess and I have to get myself out."

Note that your probes need not be restricted to clarification of problem situations. You might want to help the client clarify some opportunity, a possible goal, a strategy, or an action. Tailor the probe to where you see the client in the overall helping process.

Probe #1

a. **Empathic statement.** _____

_____

_____

b. **Issue to be explored more fully.** _____

_____

c. **Why this area?** _____

_____

d. **Possible probe.** _____

_____

Probe #2

a. **Empathic statement.** _____

_____

_____

b. **Issue to be explored more fully.** _____

_____

c. **Why this issue?** _____

_____

d. **Possible probe.** _____

_____

2. You are a counselor in a halfway house. You are dealing with Tom, 44, who has just been released from prison where he served two years for armed robbery. He has been living at the halfway house for two weeks. That is the only offense for which he has ever been convicted. The halfway house experience is designed to help him reintegrate himself into society. Living in the house is voluntary. The immediate problem is that Tom came in drunk a couple of nights ago. He was supposed to be out on a job-search day. Drinking is against the rules of the house. When you talk to him, he mumbles vaguely something about "still being confused."

Probe #1

a. **Empathic statement.** _____

_____

_____

b. **Issue to be explored more fully.** _____

_____

c. **Why this issue?** _____

_____

d. **Possible probe.** _____

_____

Probe #2

a. **Empathic statement.** _____

_____

_____

b. **Issue to be explored more fully.** _____

_____

c. **Why this issue?** _____

_____

d. **Possible probe.** _____

_____

3. Arnie is a born-again Christian. He has begun to do a fair amount of preaching at his place of employment. While some of his co-workers sympathize with his views, others are turned off. Since he feels that he is being driven by a "clear vision," he becomes more and more militant. His supervisor has cautioned him a couple of times, but this has done little to change Arnie's behavior. Finally, he is given an ultimatum to talk to one of the counselor's in the Employee Assistance Program about these issues or be suspended from his job. He says to the counselor, "I have a duty to spread the word. And if I have a duty to do so, then I also have the right. I'm a good worker. In fact, I believe in hard work. So it's not like I'm taking time off for the Lord's work. Now what's wrong with that?"

Probe #1

a. **Empathic statement.** _____

_____

b. **Issue to be explored more fully.** _____

_____

c. **Why this issue?** _____

_____

d. **Possible probe.** _____

_____

Probe #2

a. **Empathic statement.** _____

_____

_____

b. **Issue to be explored more fully.** _____

_____

c. **Why this issue?** _____

_____

d. **Possible probe.** _____

_____

Share what you have written with two other members of your training group. Get and give feedback on the accuracy of the empathy expressed. What differences do you find in the probes used? What can be learned from these differences?

EXERCISE 18: COMBINING EMPATHY WITH PROBES FOR CLARITY AND CLIENT ACTION

This exercise asks you to combine several skills--the ability to be empathic, to identify areas needing clarification, and to use probes to make clients aware of the need for action.

1. First reply to the client with empathy.
2. Identify an area needing exploration and clarification.
3. Use a probe to help the client explore or clarify some issue.
4. On the assumption that you have spent time understanding the client and helping him or her explore the problem situation through empathy and probes, indicate what action possibilities you might probe for.

Example 1

A law student, 25, is talking to a school counselor: "I learned yesterday that I've flunked out of school and that there's no recourse. I've seen everybody, but the door is shut tight. What a mess! I know I haven't gotten down to business the way I should. This is my first year in a large city and there are so many distractions. And school is so competitive. I have no idea how I'll face my parents. They've paid for my college education and this year of law school. And now I'll have to tell them that it's all down the drain."

a. **Empathy.** The whole situation sounds pretty desperate both here and at home. And it sounds so final.

b. **An area for probing.** Whom did he actually see and precisely what kinds of refusals did he get?

c. **Probe for clarity.** "I'm not sure who you mean by 'everybody' and what doors were actually shut."

d. **Probes for action possibilities.** Could he make further appeals? What advice would he give his brother if he were in this mess? How can he cut his losses? What might an honest appeal to his parents look like?

1. A high school senior to a school counselor: "My dad told me the other night that I looked relaxed. Well, I don't feel relaxed. There's a lull right now, because of semester break, but next semester I'm signed up for two math courses, and math really rips me up. But I need it for science since I want to go into pre-med."

Empathy. _____

_____

Fruitful area for probing. _____

_____

Probe. _____

_____

Probes for action possibilities. _____

_____

_____

2. A woman, 27, talking to a counselor about a relationship that has just ended (she speaks in a rather matter-of-fact voice): "I came back from visiting my parents who live in Nevada and found a letter from Gary. He said that he still loves me but that I'm just not the person for him. In the letter he thanked me for all the good times we had together these last three years. He asked me not to try to contact him because this would only make it more difficult for both of us. End of story."

Empathy. _____

_____

Fruitful area for probing. _____

_____

Probe. _____

_____

Probes for action possibilities. _____

_____

_____

3. A married man, 25, talking to a counselor about trouble with his mother-in-law: "The way I see it, she is really trying to destroy our marriage. She's so conniving. And she's very clever. It's hard to catch her in what she's doing. You know, it's rather subtle. Well, I've had it! If she's trying to destroy our marriage, she's getting pretty close to achieving her goal."

Empathy. _____

_____

Fruitful area for probing. _____

_____

Probe. _____

_____

Probes for action possibilities. _____

_____

_____

4. A woman, 31, talking to an older woman friend: "I just can't stand my job any more! My boss is so unreasonable. He makes all sorts of silly demands on me. The other women in the office are so stuffy, you can't even talk to them. The men are either very blah or after you all the time, you know, on the make. The pay is good, but I don't think it makes up for all the rest. It's been going on like this for almost two years."

Empathy. _____

_____

Fruitful area for probing. _____

_____

Probe. _____

_____

Probes for action possibilities. _____

_____

_____

5. A man, 45, who has lost his wife and home in a tornado, has been talking about his loss to a social worker: "This happened to a friend of mine in Kansas about ten years ago. He never recovered from it. His life just disintegrated and nobody could do anything about it. . . . It was like the end of the world for him. You never think it's going to happen to you. I know I belong here. But this kind of thing makes me think I don't."

Empathy. _____

_____

Fruitful area for probing. _____

_____

Probe. _____

_____

Probes for action possibilities. _____

_____

_____

6. A divorced woman, 44, talking to a counselor about her drinking. This is the second session. She has spent a lot of time telling her story. To the counselor there seemed to be a lot of evasions and some outright lying: "Actually, it's a relief to tell someone. I don't have to give you any excuses or make the story sound right. I drink because I like to drink; I'm just crazy about the stuff, that's all. But I'm under no delusions that telling you is going to solve anything. When I get out of here, I know I'm going straight to a bar and drink. Some new bar, new faces, some place they don't know me."

Empathy. _____

_____

Fruitful area for probing. _____

_____

Probe. _____

_____

Probes for action possibilities. _____

7. A man, 57, talking to a counselor about a family problem: "My younger brother, he's 53, has always been a kind of bum. He's always poaching off the rest of the family. Last week my unmarried sister told me that she'd given him some money for a 'business deal.' Business deal, my foot! I'd like to get hold of him and kick his ass! Oh, he's not a vicious guy. Just weak. He's never been able to get a fix on life. But he's got the whole family in turmoil now, and we can't keep going through hell for him."

Empathy. _____

_____

Fruitful area for probing. _____

_____

Probe. _____

_____

Probes for action possibilities. _____

_____

8. A woman, 49, talking to a counselor about her relationship with her husband: "To put it frankly, my husband isn't very interested in me sexually any more. We've had sex maybe once or twice in the last two or three months. What makes it worse is that I still have very strong sexual feelings. It seems they're even stronger than they used to be. I keep thinking about this all the time. He doesn't seem very interested at all. I don't know if he's got someone on the side. I'm not handling it well."

Empathy. _____

_____

Fruitful area for probing. _____

_____

Probe. _____

_____

Probes for action possibilities. _____

_____

_____

9. A man, 49, talking to a rehabilitation counselor after an operation that has left him with one lung: "I'll never be as active as I used to be. But at least I'm beginning to see that life is still

worth living. I have to take a long look at the possibilities, no matter how much they've narrowed. I can't explain it, but there's something good stirring in me."

Empathy. _____

_____

Fruitful area for probing. _____

_____

Probe. _____

_____

Probes for action possibilities. _____

_____

_____

10. Mark and Lisa, a married couple, both 33, after years of attempting to have children finally adopted a baby girl, Andrea. Their relationship, which up to then seemed quite good, has begun to disintegrate. Mark has made some cracks about "the stronger one in the house." Andrea has proved to be a somewhat difficult baby. Lisa feels exhausted and blames Mark for not helping her. They are both thinking about divorce now, but feel very guilty because of the child. Both of them say, "If only we had never adopted Andrea."

Empathy. _____

_____

Fruitful area for probing. _____

_____

Probe. _____

_____

Probes for action possibilities. _____

_____

_____

PART FOUR

STAGE I: IDENTIFYING AND CLARIFYING PROBLEM SITUATIONS

Here we begin with exercises related directly to the stages and steps of the helping model. The overall purpose of the exercises in Part Four is to help you develop the kinds of skills that will enable you to help clients:

* identify and clarify problem situations and missed opportunities
* challenge themselves to develop new and more useful perspectives on themselves and their problems.
* work on key issues, that is, issues that will make a difference in their lives.
* commit themselves to work on these issues in pragmatic, action-oriented ways.

The exercises in Part Four relate to the three steps of Stage I. However, as indicated in the text, the tasks of Stage-I steps are not only interrelated but apply to all stages and steps of the helping process.

STEP I-A: HELPING CLIENTS TELL THEIR STORIES

The communication skills reviewed in Part Three will help you deliver the stages and steps of the helping model. Stage I deals with problem identification and clarification. Step A in this stage deals with helping clients tell their stories, that is, discuss the problem situations, anxieties, and concerns that bring them (or get them sent) to the helper in the first place.

Reviewing Your Own Concerns

The exercises in this section are designed to help you tell your own story, that is, to help you identify the issues, problems, and concerns of your own life that might stand in the way of helping others. Thoughtful execution of some of the exercises in this section will give you a list of issues, neither too superficial nor too intimate, to discuss and work on in the training group. The training program is a golden opportunity for you to grow and develop.

Focusing on the issues that might stand in the way of being a skilled helper with your clients is in keeping with the values of competence, pragmatism, genuineness, and self-responsibility discussed in Chapter Three of the text. Later on some of these exercises can be used with clients to help them identify and clarify their concerns.

Here, in statement form, are some of the kinds of problems, issues, and concerns that trainees have dealt with during training programs.

* I'm shy. My shyness takes the form of being afraid to meet strangers and being afraid to reveal myself to others.
* I'm a fairly compliant person. Others can push me around and get away with it.
* I get angry fairly easily and let my anger spill out on others in irresponsible ways. I think my anger is often linked to not getting my own way.
* I'm a lazy person. I find it especially difficult to expend the kind of energy necessary to listen to and get involved with others.
* I'm somewhat fearful of persons of the opposite sex. This is especially true if I think they are putting some kind of demand on me for closeness. I get nervous and try to get away.
* I'm a rather insensitive person, or so I have been told. I'm a kind of bull-in-the-china-shop type. Not much tact.
* I'm overly controlled. I don't let my emotions show very much. Sometimes I don't even want to know what I'm feeling myself.
* I like to control others, but I like to do so in subtle ways. I want to stay in charge of interpersonal relationships at all times.
* I have a strong need to be liked by others. I seldom do anything that might offend others or that others would not approve of. I have a very strong need to be accepted.
* I have few positive feelings about myself. I put myself down in a variety of ways. I get depressed a lot.
* I never stop to examine my values. I think I hold some conflicting values. I'm not even sure why I'm interested in becoming a helper.
* I feel almost compelled to help others. It's part of my religious background. It's as if I didn't even have a choice.
* I'm sensitive and easily hurt. I think I send out messages to others that say "be careful of me."
* I'm overly dependent on others. My self-image depends too much on what others think of me.
* A number of people see me as a "difficult" person. I'm highly individualistic. I'm ready to fight if anyone imposes on my freedom.
* I'm anxious a lot of the time. I'm not even sure why. My palms sweat a lot in interpersonal situations.
* I see myself as a rather colorless, uninteresting person. I'm bored with myself at times and I assume that others are bored with me.
* I'm somewhat irresponsible. I take too many risks, especially risks that involve others. I'm very impulsive. That's probably a nice way of saying that I lack self-control.
* I'm very stubborn. I have fairly strong opinions. I argue a lot and try to get others to see things my way. I argue about very little things.
* I don't examine myself or my behavior very much. I'm usually content with the way things are. I don't expect too much of myself or of others.
* I can be sneaky in my relationships with others. I seduce people in different ways--not necessarily sexual--by my "charm." I get them to do what I want.
* I like the good life. I'm pretty materialistic and I like my own comfort. I don't often go out of my way to meet the needs of others.
* I'm somewhat lonely. I don't think others like me, if they think about me at all. I spend time feeling sorry for myself.
* I'm awkward in social situations. I don't do the right thing at the right time. I don't know what others are feeling when I'm with them and I guess I seem callous.
* Others see me as "out of it" a great deal of the time. I guess I am fairly naive. Others seem to have deeper or more interesting experiences than I do. I think I've grown up too

sheltered.

* I'm stingy with both money and time. I don't want to share what I have with others. I'm pretty selfish.
* I'm somewhat of a coward. I sometimes find it hard to stand up for my convictions even when I meet light opposition. It's easy to get me to retreat.
* I hate conflict. I'm more or less a peace-at-any-price person. I run when things get heated up.
* I don't like it when others tell me I'm doing something wrong. I usually feel attacked and I attack back.

This list is not exhaustive, but you can use it to stimulate your thinking about yourself and the kinds of dissatisfactions, problems, or concerns you may have about yourself, especially concerns that might relate to your effectiveness as a helper. The exercises in Step I-A will help you assess your satisfactions and dissatisfactions with yourself and your behavior. You can then choose the issues that you would like to explore during the training sessions.

STRENGTHS AND SOFT SPOTS

All of us have strengths and soft spots, areas in which we could use some improvement. I might well be a decisive person and that is a strength for me as a helper but, in being decisive, I might push others too hard and that is a soft spot needing improvement. In this case, a strength pushed too hard becomes a soft spot.

EXERCISE 19: STRENGTHS AND SOFT SPOTS IN MY LIFE

Sometimes a very simple structure can help you and your clients identify the major dimensions of a problem situation. This exercise asks you to identify some of the things that are not going as well as you would like them to go in your life and some of the things you believe you are handling well. It is important right from the beginning to help clients become aware of their resources and successes as well as their problems and failures. Problems can be handled more easily if they are seen in the wider context of resources and successes.

In this exercise, merely jot down in whatever way they come to you things that are going right and things that could be going better for you. In order to stress the positive, see if you can write down at least two things that are going right for every thing that needs improvement. Read the list in the example that follows and then do your own. Don't worry whether the problems or concerns you list are really important. Jot down whatever comes to your mind. Your own list may include items similar to those in the example, but it may be quite different because it will reflect you and not someone else.

Example

Strengths	Soft Spots
I have a lot of friends.	I seem to have a very negative attitude toward myself.
I have a decent job and people like the do.	I get dependent on others much too easily. work I
Others can count on me; I'm dependable	My life seems boring too much of the time
I have a reasonable amount of intelligence	I am afraid to take risks
I have no major financial difficulties; I'm secure.	
My wife and I get along fairly well.	
I am very healthy.	
My belief in God gives me a kind of center in life, a stability.	

53

Strengths	Soft Spots
_____	_____
_____	_____
_____	_____
_____	_____
_____	_____
_____	_____
_____	_____
_____	_____
_____	_____
_____	_____

DEVELOPMENTAL TASKS

Many of the clients you see will be struggling with developmental concerns like those you have struggled with or are currently working on. Like you, they will have both strengths and "soft spots" in coping with the developmental tasks of life.

EXERCISE 20: REVIEWING SOME BASIC DEVELOPMENTAL TASKS

In this exercise you are asked to consider your experience with ten major developmental tasks of life. First reflect on your experience in these developmental areas and then apply what you have learned to your role as a helper of others. Use extra paper as needed.

1. **COMPETENCE. What do I do well?** Do I see myself as a person who is capable of getting things done? Do I have the resources needed to accomplish goals I set for myself? In what areas of life do I excel? In what areas of life would I want to be more competent than I am?

Strengths	Soft Spots
_____	_____
_____	_____

2. **AUTONOMY: Can I make it on my own?**   Can I get things done on my own? Do I avoid being overly dependent or independent? Am I reasonably interdependent in my work and social life? When I need help, do I find it easy to ask for it? In what social settings do I find myself most dependent? counterdependent? independent? interdependent?

<table>
<tr><td align="center">Strengths</td><td align="center">Soft Spots</td></tr>
<tr><td></td><td></td></tr>
<tr><td></td><td></td></tr>
<tr><td></td><td></td></tr>
<tr><td></td><td></td></tr>
</table>

3. **VALUES: What do I believe in?**   What are my principal values? Do I allow for reasonable changes in my value system? Do I put my values into practice? Do any of the values I hold conflict with others? In what social settings do I pursue the values that are most important to me?

<table>
<tr><td align="center">Strengths</td><td align="center">Soft Spots</td></tr>
<tr><td></td><td></td></tr>
<tr><td></td><td></td></tr>
<tr><td></td><td></td></tr>
<tr><td></td><td></td></tr>
</table>

4. **IDENTITY: Who am I in this world?**   Do I have a good sense of who I am and the direction I'm going in life? Do the ways that others see me fit with the ways in which I see myself? Do I have some kind of center that gives meaning to my life? In what social settings do I have my best feelings for who I am? In what social settings do I lose my identity? In what ways am I confused or dissatisfied with who I am?

<table>
<tr><td align="center">Strengths</td><td align="center">Soft Spots</td></tr>
<tr><td></td><td></td></tr>
<tr><td></td><td></td></tr>
<tr><td></td><td></td></tr>
<tr><td></td><td></td></tr>
</table>

5. **INTIMACY. What are my closer relationships like?**   What kinds of closeness do I have

with others? To what extent are there degrees of closeness in my life--acquaintances, friends, and intimates? What is my life in my peer group like? How well do I get along with others? What concerns do I have about my interpersonal life?

Strengths	Soft Spots
_____	_____
_____	_____
_____	_____
_____	_____

6. **SEXUALITY. Who am I as a sexual person?**   To what degree am I satisfied with my sexual identity, my sexual preferences, and my sexual behavior? How do I handle my sexual needs and wants? What social settings influence the ways I act sexually?

Strengths	Soft Spots
_____	_____
_____	_____
_____	_____
_____	_____

7. **LOVE, MARRIAGE, FAMILY. What are my deeper commitments like?** What is my marriage like? How do I relate to family and relatives? How do I feel about the quality of my family life? If not married, in what ways do I look forward to marriage? What misgivings do I have?

Strengths	Soft Spots
_____	_____
_____	_____
_____	_____
_____	_____

8. **CAREER. What is the place of work in my life?** How do I feel about the way I am preparing myself for a career or the career I am currently pursuing? What do I get out of work? What am I like in the workplace? How does it affect me? What impact do I have there?

Strengths	Soft Spots
_____	_____
_____	_____
_____	_____
_____	_____

9. **INVESTMENT IN THE WIDER COMMUNITY. How big is my world?** How do I invest myself in the world outside of friends, work, and the family? What is my neighborhood like? Do I have community, civic, political, social involvements or concerns? In what ways am I optimistic about the world? In what ways am I cynical?

Strengths	Soft Spots
_____	_____
_____	_____
_____	_____
_____	_____

10. **LEISURE. What do I do with my free time?** Do I feel that I have sufficient free time? How do I use my leisure? What do I get out of it? In what social settings do I spend my free time?

Strengths	Soft Spots
_____	_____
_____	_____
_____	_____
_____	_____

Many of the clients you see will be struggling with similar developmental concerns. Like you, they will have both strengths and "soft spots" in these areas.

In your opinion, which of the strengths you have noted will help you be a more effective counselor? In what specific ways?

_____

_____

_____

_____

_____

_____

_____

_____

_____

_____

_____

_____

In your opinion, which of the soft spots you have noted might stand in the way of your being an effective helper? In what specific ways?

_____

_____

_____

_____

_____

THE SOCIAL SETTINGS OF LIFE

We belong to and participate in a number of different social settings in life: family, circle of friends, clubs, church groups, school groups, and the like. We are also affected by what goes on in our neighborhoods and the cities and towns in which we live. Larger systems, such as state and national governments, have their ways of entering our lives. We manage some of our interactions in these settings quite well, we have soft spots in others.

EXERCISE 21: CONFLICTS IN THE SOCIAL SETTINGS OF LIFE

This is another exercise that will help you review areas in which clients have problems and also help you identify strengths and soft spots that relate to your role as helper.

1. **Chart the social settings of life.** Since you are a member of a number of different social settings and since each places certain demands on you, conflicts can arise between settings. In this exercise you are asked to write you name in the middle of a sheet of paper. Then, as in the example (Figure 2), draw spokes out to the various social settings of your life. The person in the example is Mitch, 45, a principal of an inner-city high school in a large city. He is married and has two teenage sons. Neither attends the high school of which he is principal. He is seeing a counselor because of exhaustion and bouts of hostility and depression. He has had a complete physical check-up and there is no evidence of any medical problem.

58

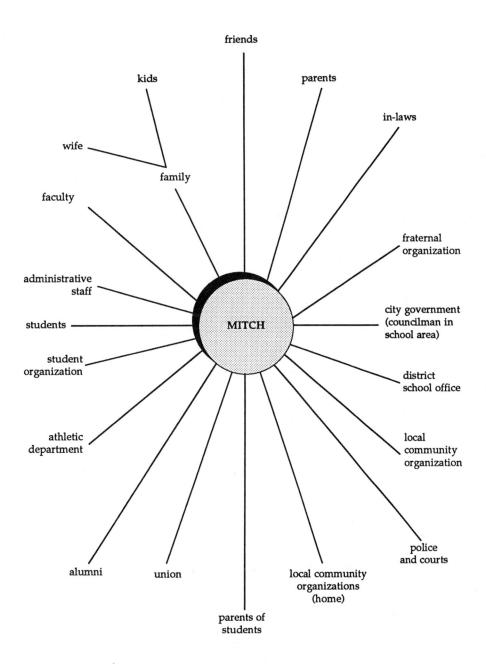

Figure 2. Chart of Social Settings

2. **Review expectations, demands, concerns.** Now take each social setting and write down the expectations people have of you in that setting, the demands they place on you, the concerns you have, the dissatisfactions expressed to you. For instance, some of things Mitch writes are:

Faculty

* Some faculty members want a personal relationship with me and I have neither the time nor the desire.
* Some faculty members have retired on the job. I don't know what to do with them.
* Some of the white faculty members are suspicious of me and distant just because I'm black.
* One faculty member wrote the district superintendent and said that I was undermining her reputation with other faculty members. This is not true.

Family

* My wife says that I'm letting school consume me; she complains constantly because I don't spend enough time at home.
* My kids seem to withdraw from me because I'm a double authority figure, a father and a principal.

Parents

* My mother is infirm; my retired father calls me and tells me what a hard time he's having getting used to retirement.
* My mother tells me not to be spending time with her when I have so much to do and then she complains to my wife and my father when I don't show up.

Mitch goes on to list demands, expectations, concerns, and frustrations that relate to each of the settings he has listed on his chart.

On a separate sheet of paper, list the demands, expectations, and concerns related to each of the social settings you have on your chart. Do not try to solve any of the problems you see cropping up. If some solution to a problem does suggest itself while you are doing this exercise, jot it down and put it aside.

3. **Identify conflicts between systems.** Once you review the expectations, demands, and concerns associated with each setting, list the conflicts between settings that cause you concern. Here are some of the conflicts Mitch identifies:

* My wife wants me to spend more time at home and yet she criticizes me for not spending more time with my parents.

* The students, both individually and through their organizations, keep asking me to be more liberal while their parents are asking me to tighten things up.
* My administrative staff thinks that I'm taking sides against them in a dispute with the athletic department.
* My friends say that I spend so much time at work involving myself in crisis management that I have no time left for them; they tell me I'm doing myself in.

Conflicts Between the Social Settings of My Life

_____

_____

_____

_____

_____

_____

_____

_____

4. **Themes.** Share with the other members of your training group the kinds of conflicts you have identified. What kinds of themes emerge?

5. **Action.** Choose one conflict and identify some of the things you might do to resolve it. For instance, Mitch, in talking about the conflict between his work and his friends, decides to use the "overfull calendar" technique. That is, he puts social gatherings into his calendar. Then, when others ask for his time, he tells them what times are already taken and asks them to choose from the times that are left. Of course, he does not say that a certain day is taken up with an outing with friends.

a. **The conflict.** _____

_____

b. **Possible actions.** _____

_____

_____

_____

_____

LIFE SKILLS

Sometimes people develop problems or fail to manage them very well because they do not have the kinds of **life skills** needed to handle developmental tasks and to invest themselves effectively in the social systems of life. For instance, a young married couple, Roger and Tess, find that they don't have the communication skills needed to talk to each other reasonably about the problems they have been encountering during the first couple of years of marriage.

EXERCISE 22: ASSESSING WORKING KNOWLEDGE AND SKILLS FOR EFFECTIVE LIVING

This exercise is a checklist designed to help you get in touch with both your resources and possible areas of deficit. Listed below are various groups of skills needed to undertake the tasks of everyday living. Rate yourself on each skill. The rating system is as follows:

5. I have a **very high** level of this skill.   /
4. I have a **moderately high** level of this skill.
3. From what I can judge, I am about **average** in this skill.

3. From what I can judge, I am about **average** in this skill.
2. I have a **moderate deficit** in this skill.
1. I have a **serious deficit** in this skill.

You are also asked to rate how important each skill is in your eyes. Use the following scale.

5. For me this skill is **very important**.
4. For me this skill is of **moderate** importance.
3. For me this skill has **average** importance.
2. For me this skill is **rather unimportant**.
1. For me this skill is **not** important at all.

1. **Body-Related Skills**	Level	Importance
* Knowing how to put together nutritional meals.	——	——
* Knowing how to control weight.	——	——
* Knowing how to keep fit through exercise.	——	——
* Knowing how to maintain basic body hygiene.	——	——
* Basic grooming skills.	——	——
* Knowing what to do when everyday health problems such as colds and minor accidents occur.	——	——
* Skills related to sexual expression.	——	——
* Athletic skills.	——	——
* Aesthetic skills such as dancing.	——	——

Other body-related skills:

	Level	Importance
* _____	——	——
* _____	——	——

2. **Learning-How-to-Learn Skills**	Level	Importance
* Knowing how to read well.	——	——
* Knowing how to write clearly.	——	——
* Knowing basic mathematics.	——	——
* Knowing how to learn and study efficiently.	——	——
* Knowing something about the use of computers.	——	——
* Using history to understand today's events.	——	——
* Being able to use basic statistics.	——	——
* Knowing how to use a library.	——	——
* Knowing how to find information I need.	——	——

Other learning and learning-how-to-learn skills.

	Level	Importance
* _____	——	——
* _____	——	——
* _____	——	

3. **Skills Related to Values**	Level	Importance
* Knowing how to clarify my own values.	——	——
* Knowing how to identify the values of others who have a significant relationship to me.	——	——

	Level	Importance
* Knowing how to identify the values being "pushed" by the social systems to which I belong.	____	____
* Knowing how to construct and reconstruct my own set of values.	____	____

Other value-related skills:

* _____	____	____
* _____	____	____
* _____	____	____

4. Self-Management Skills

	Level	Importance
* Knowing how to plan and set realistic goals.	____	____
* Problem-solving or problem-management skills.	____	____
* Decision-making skills.	____	____
* Knowing and being able to use basic principles of behavior such as the use of incentives.	____	____
* Knowing how to manage my emotions.	____	____
* Knowing how to delay gratification.	____	____
* Assertiveness: knowing how to get my needs met while respecting the legitimate needs of others.	____	____

Other self-management skills:

* _____	____	____
* _____	____	____
* _____	____	____

5. Communication Skills

	Level	Importance
* The ability to speak before a group.	____	____
* The ability to listen to others actively.	____	____
* The ability to understand others.	____	____
* The ability to communicate understanding to others (empathy).	____	____
* The ability to challenge others reasonably.	____	____
* The ability to provide useful information to others.	____	____
* The ability to explore with another person what is happening in my relationship to him or her.	____	____

Other communication skills:

* _____	____	____
* _____	____	____
* _____	____	____

6. Skills Related to Small Groups

* Knowing how to be an effective, active member of	____	____

a small group.
* Knowing how to design and organize a group.   ____ ____
* Knowing how to lead a small group.   ____ ____
* Team-building skills.   ____ ____

Other small-group skills:

* _____   ____ ____

* _____   ____ ____

* _____   ____ ____

    Now that you have done a brief assessment of some life skills, indicate which skills, if improved, would help you manage your concerns, problems, or soft spots better. When you name a skill, indicate why such a skill is important to you and what you might do to develop it.

_____

_____

_____

_____

_____

_____

_____

_____

_____

    What kinds of life skills do you think you need to become better at, not just to handle your own problems more effectively, but to be an effective counselor?

_____

_____

_____

_____

_____

_____

_____

GENERAL STRENGTHS AND SOFT SPOTS

The next two sentence-completion exercises are designed to help you further review both soft spots and strengths.

EXERCISE 23: A SENTENCE-COMPLETION ASSESSMENT OF PERSONAL PROBLEMS

Do these sentence-completion exercises quickly. They may help you expand in more specific ways what you have learned about yourself in the preceding exercises.

1. My biggest problem is _____

_____

2. I'm quite concerned about _____

_____

3. One of my other problems is _____

_____

4. Something I do that gives me trouble is _____

_____

5. Something I fail to do that gets me into trouble is _____

_____

6. The social setting of life I find most troublesome is _____

_____

7. The most frequent negative feelings in my life are _____

_____

8. These negative feelings take place when _____

_____

9. The person I have most trouble with is _____

_____

10. What I find most troublesome in this relationship is _____

11. Life would be better if _____

12. I tend to do myself in when I _____

13. I don't cope very well with _____

14. What sets me most on edge is _____

15. I get anxious when _____

16. A value I fail to put into practice is _____

17. I'm afraid to _____

18. I wish I _____

19. I wish I didn't _____

20. What others dislike most about me is _____

21. What I don't seem to handle well is _____

22. I don't seem to have the skills I need in order to _____

23. A problem that keeps coming back is _____

24. If I could change just one thing in myself it would be _____

_____

EXERCISE 24: A SENTENCE-COMPLETION ASSESSMENT OF STRENGTHS

1. One thing I like about myself is _____

_____

2. One thing others like about me is _____

_____

3. One thing I do very well is _____

_____

4. A recent problem I've handled very well is _____

_____

5. When I'm at my best I _____

_____

6. I'm glad that I am able to _____

_____

7. Those who know me know that I can _____

_____

8. A compliment that has been paid to me recently is _____

_____

9. A value that I try hard to practice is _____

_____

10. An example of my caring about others is _____

_____

11. People can count on me to _____

_____

12. They said I did a good job when I _____

_____

13. Something I'm handling better this year than last is _____

_____

14. One thing that I've overcome is _____

_____

15. A good example of my ability to manage my life is _____

_____

16. I'm best with people when _____

_____

17. One goal I'm presently working toward is _____

_____

18. A recent temptation that I managed to overcome was _____

_____

19. I pleasantly surprised myself when I _____

_____

20. I think that I have the guts to _____

_____

21. If I had to say one good thing about myself I'd say that I _____

_____

22. One way I successfully control my emotions is _____

_____

23. One way in which I am very dependable is _____

_____

24. One important thing I intend to do within the next two months is _____

_____

EXERCISE 25: USING STRENGTHS TO MANAGE SOFT SPOTS

Sometimes we fail to see that our strengths provide the resources we need to manage areas in our lives needing improvement. In this exercise you are asked to relate resources to problems or undeveloped opportunities in your life.

1. List two of your key concerns or problems.
2. After each, list the resources you've identified in yourself that can help you manage your problem more effectively. Try to name resources that you are not currently using to manage the particular problem area.

Example

Katrina, a trainee in her late 20s, is concerned about bouts of anxiety. She has led a rather sheltered life and now realizes that she needs to "break out" in a number of ways if she is to be an effective counselor. The fact that she has been sheltered from so much is at the root of her anxiety. The counseling program has put her in touch with all sorts of people, and this is anxiety provoking. She lists some of the strengths she has that can help her overcome her anxiety.

* I'm bright. I know that a great deal of my anxiety comes from fear of the unknown.
* I'm intellectually adventuresome. I pursue new ideas. Perhaps this can help me be more adventuresome in seeking new experiences. New ideas don't kill me. I bet new experiences won't either.
* People find me easy to talk to. This can help me form friendships. My fears have kept me from developing friendships. However, developing more relationships is the royal route to the kinds of experiences I need.
* At root, I'm a religious person. This can help me put my fears into a larger context. In the larger context they seem petty.

Apply the same procedure to your two concerns.

Concern #1. _____

_____

Strengths that can be used to manage this concern. _____

_____

_____

Concern #2. _____

_____

Strengths that can be used to manage this concern. _____

_____

_____

STEP I-B: CHALLENGING:

HELPING CLIENTS MANAGE BLIND SPOTS AND DEVELOP NEW PERSPECTIVES

Challenging skills include information sharing, advanced empathy, helper self-sharing, and immediacy. The purpose of these skills is to help clients get in touch with blind spots and develop the kind of new perspectives or behavioral insights needed to complete the clarification of a problem situation and to move on to developing new scenarios, setting problem-managing goals, developing strategies, and moving to action. Challenging skills and processes are useful to the degree that they serve the stages and steps of the helping process.

INFORMATION GIVING

As noted in the text, sometimes clients do not get a clear picture of a problem situation or manage it more effectively because they lack information needed for clarity and action. Information can provide clients with some of the new perspectives they need to see problem situations as manageable. Giving clients problem-clarifying information or helping them find it themselves is not, of course, the same as advice giving or preaching.

EXERCISE 26: USEFUL INFORMATION FOR MANAGING YOUR OWN PROBLEMS

In this exercise you are asked to review the problem areas you have chosen to deal with during this training program. Choose two areas and ask yourself whether there is some kind of information that would help you understand your problem more thoroughly or help you do something to manage it more effectively.

Example

Jess, a counselor trainee, 30, has been married a little over a year. He has just quit work to start full time in school in a counselor training program. He is having trouble with his marriage. He is having second thoughts about quitting his job and entering the program. He has had no background in psychology previous to this. In college he majored in history. In doing this exercise, he came up with the following:

"What kind of information would help me see my concerns more clearly?

* I need information about what job opportunities there are for people like myself with an M.A. in counseling psychology. This will help me to commit myself to the program more fully.
* It would be helpful for me (and my wife) to know more about what kinds of pitfalls exist for a couple in the first two years of marriage. I have a feeling that some of the problems we are having are not uncommon for 'beginners.'
* I don't know what the normative developmental challenges are for someone my age. My wife is 24. We are at different stages. She seems to be going through stuff I've already seen. I feel uprooted. Some applied developmental psychology would help me.

Now that I write this down, it's clear that I can get a lot of this information for myself as part of this program."

Jess found some of the information challenging. For instance, it was disturbing to learn that many people in the helping professions considered the M.A. a second-class degree, while for him it would be quite an achievement. He knew that he would have to talk to M.A. graduates working in helping settings to see this issue through their eyes. He also knew that he had to find out what the future held for helpers with an M.A.

1. Choose two areas you are working on and ask yourself what kind of information would help you see yourself and your problem situation more clearly and do something about managing it.
2. In a small-group forum established by your instructor, share what you have learned in one of the two areas you have worked on.

Problem area #1 _____

_____

Information needed _____

_____

_____

_____

_____

_____

_____

Problem area #2 _____

_____

Information needed _____

_____

_____

_____

_____

_____

_____

In groups of three, share one of your problem areas and what kind of information you believe will help you manage it more effectively. Can either of your fellow trainees help you with the information you need? Do either of them fall into the trap of advice giving or preaching? What did you learn about yourself or the helping process that could be jotted down in your journal?

EXERCISE 27: INFORMATION AND NEW PERSPECTIVES

In this exercise you are asked to consider what kind of information you might give or help clients get that would help them see the problem situations they are facing more clearly. Information can, somewhat artificially, be divided into two kinds: (a) information that helps clients understand their difficulties better, and (b) information about what actions they might take.

Example

Tim was a bright, personable young man. During college he was hospitalized after taking a drug overdose during a bout of depression. He spent six months as an in-patient. He was assigned to "milieu therapy," an amorphous mixture of work and recreation designed more to keep patients busy than to help them grapple with their problems and engage in constructive changes. He was given drugs for his depression, seen occasionally by a psychiatrist, and assigned to a therapy group that proved to be quite aimless. After leaving the hospital, his confidence shattered, he left college and got involved with a variety of low-paying, part-time jobs. He finally finished college by going to night school, but he avoided full-time jobs for fear of being asked about his past. Buried inside him was the thought, "I have this terrible secret that I have to keep from everyone." A friend talked him into taking a college-sponsored communication-skills course one summer. The psychologist running the program, noting Tim's rather substantial natural talents together with his self-effacing ways, remarked to him one day, "I wonder what kind of ambitions you have." In an instant Tim realized that he had buried all thoughts of ambition. After all, he didn't "deserve" to be ambitious. Tim, instinctively trusting him, divulged his "terrible secret" for the first time.

Tim and the psychologist had a number of meetings over the next few years. Challenge became an important part of the helping process. In some of the early sessions, Rick, Tim's counselor, provided him with information that proved challenging in a number of areas.

* that Tim is probably more intelligent and talented than he realizes, that he is underemployed,
* that employers do not necessarily dig deeply into the background of prospective employees,
* that privacy laws protect him from damaging disclosures,
* that many employers look benignly on the pecadillos and developmental crises of a prospective employee's adolescent years,
* that the job market is strong and growing stronger so that people with Tim's skills and potential are in high demand.

Of course, Rick did not dump all of this information on Tim in the first session. In fact, he encouraged Tim to dig out some of the information--for instance, the strength of the job market--on his own. This kind of information challenged Tim's views of himself, his assumptions about his past, and his ambitionless lifestyle.

In the following cases you are not asked to be an expert. Rather, from a lay person's or a common-sense point of view, you are asked to indicate what kinds of information you believe might help the client understand and manage the problem situation more clearly. Specific, expert information is not called for. What blind spots do you think the client has? How do you think information might help? In what ways would the information be challenging?

1. A man, 26, has just been sentenced to five years in a penitentiary. He is talking to a chaplain-counselor who has worked for the past ten years at the penitentiary to which the man has been assigned. The chaplain also counseled the man during his trial. The man is deathly afraid of going to prison and has even talked about taking his own life.

What kinds of information might help this client understand/act?

_____

_____

_____

_____

_____

_____

2. A woman, 45, has learned that she has cancer and will soon undergo a mastectomy. She has been put in touch with a self-help group composed of women who have had this operation. She is now talking to one of the members of this group.

What kinds of information might help this client understand/act?

_____

_____

_____

_____

_____

3. A woman, 28, has been raped and is talking to a counselor at a rape-counseling center. The rape happened two hours ago. She has not yet reported the rape to the police.

What kinds of information might help this client understand/act?

_____

_____

_____

_____

_____

4. A man, 34, comes for counseling because he fears his drinking might be getting out of hand. He's been drinking heavily for several years and recently has had some physical symptoms that he hasn't experienced before, for instance, blackouts. He has managed to remain a secret drinker. At his job he works by himself and has not had more "sick" days than the average. None of his immediate family or friends has been an alcoholic.

What kinds of information might help this client understand/act?

_____

_____

_____

_____

_____

_____

5. A man, 41, comes to counseling because he fears he is going crazy. He has a number of problems. His marriage has deteriorated in the past year or so. He and his wife relate poorly to each other. He sees his teenage son and daughter drifting away from him and he doesn't understand this. He fears that his son might be taking drugs on occasion but has not confronted him. He is drinking more than he should. He goes in and out of bouts of mild depression. He has begun to steal little things from stores, not because he needs them, but because "it gives him a lift."

What kinds of information might help this client understand/act?

_____

_____

_____

_____

_____

_____

6. Cindy, 23, has been bleeding internally. She is about to undergo a series of tests. She is very frightened and fears the worst. She has never been seriously sick in her life. She fears the doctors, the tests, the hospital. She has never even visited anyone in a hospital.

What kinds of information might help this client understand/act?

_____

_____

_____

_____

_____

_____

7. Tim, 18, has been smoking marijuana for about three years. He is a fairly heavy user. He has

recently received several shocks. His father died suddenly and his steady girlfriend left him. Since he was not especially close to his father, he is surprised by how hard he is hit by the loss. After reading a couple of articles on marijuana use, he developed fears that he has been doing irreversible genetic damage to himself. His is fearful of giving it up because he thinks he needs it to carry him over this period of special stress and because he fears withdrawal symptoms.

What kinds of information might help this client understand/act?

_____

_____

_____

_____

_____

_____

8. Edna, 17, is an unmarried woman who is experiencing her third unexpected and unwanted pregnancy. The other two ended in abortion. She feels guilty about the third unwanted pregnancy and about the abortions. Many of her relatives belong to a fundamentalist church. She is thinking about keeping this child. For all her promiscuity, she seems to know little about sex. She believes that men just take advantage of her.

What kinds of information might help this client understand/act?

_____

_____

_____

_____

_____

_____

9. Maxine, 54, has suffered a stroke that has left her partially paralyzed on her left side and with speech that is a bit slurred. Her husband, who seems lost without her, seems artificially cheerful during his visits. She is about to be transferred to a rehabilitation unit. She has a long road ahead of her. She is depressed.

What kinds of information might help this client understand/act?

_____

_____

_____

_____

ADVANCED EMPATHY

Advanced empathy, described most simply, means sharing **hunches** about clients and their overt and covert experiences, behaviors, and feelings that you feel will help them see their problems and concerns more clearly and help them move on to developing new scenarios, setting goals, and acting. Advanced empathy as hunch sharing can be expressed in a number of ways. Some of these are reviewed briefly below. Before doing the following exercises, however, review the section of advanced empathy in the text.

Some Approaches to Advanced Empathy

* Hunches that help clients see the **bigger picture**. Example: "The problem doesn't seem to be just your attitude toward your brother-in-law any more; your resentment seems to have spread to his friends. How do you see it?"

* Hunches that help the clients see what they are expressing **indirectly** or merely **implying**. Example: "I think I might also be hearing you say that you are more than disappointed--perhaps a bit hurt and angry."

* Hunches that help clients draw **logical conclusions** from what they are saying. Example: "From all that you've said about her, it seems that you are also saying that right now you resent having to be with her. I know you haven't said that directly. But I'm wondering if you are feeling that way about her."

* Hunches that help clients open up areas they are only **hinting** at. Example: "You've brought up sexual matters a number of times, but you haven't pursued them. My guess is that sex is a pretty important area for you but perhaps pretty touchy, too."

* Hunches that help clients see things they may be **overlooking**. Example: "I wonder if it's possible that some people take your wit too personally, that they see it as sarcasm rather than humor."

* Hunches that help clients identify **themes**. Example: "If I'm not mistaken, you've mentioned in two or three different ways that it is sometimes difficult for you to stick up for your own legitimate rights. For instance . . . ."

* Hunches that help client **own** only partially experiences, behaviors, and/or feelings. Example: "You sound as if you have already decided to marry him, but I don't think that I hear you saying that directly."

Hunches should be based on your experience of your clients--their experiences, behaviors, and emotions both within the helping sessions themselves and in their day-to-day lives. Do not base your hunches on "deep" psychological theories. Later on, you will be asked to identify the experiential and behavioral <u>clues</u> on which your hunches are based.

EXERCISE 28: TENTATIVENESS IN THE USE OF CHALLENGING SKILLS

As noted in the text, challenges are usually more effective if they do not sound like accusations. Therefore, in challenging clients, don't accuse them but don't be so tentative that the force of the challenge is lost.

1.   In the examples of the different kinds of hunches just outlined, underline the words or phrases that you think add tentativeness to the challenge.
2.   Indicate whether you believe that a useful degree of tentativeness has been expressed.
3.   List other ways in which you believe that tentativeness can be expressed (that is, other than the ways used in the examples).

Challenging, at its best, is a way of inviting clients to explore their behavior (or lack of it) in order to understand it better and to change it.

EXERCISE 29: ADVANCED ACCURATE EMPATHY--HUNCHES ABOUT ONESELF

One way to get an experiential feeling for advanced empathy is to explore at two levels some situation or issue in your own life that you would like to understand more clearly. One level of understanding could be called the surface level. The second could be called a more objective or a deeper level.

1.   Review the material on advanced accurate empathy.
2.   Read the examples given below.
3.   Choose some issue, topic, situation, or relationship that you have been investigating and which you would like to understand more fully with a view to taking some kind of action on it. As usual, choose issues that you are willing to share with the members of your training group and try to choose issues that might affect the quality of your counseling.
4.   First, briefly describe the issue, as in the examples.
5.   Then give your present "surface-level" description of the issue.
6.   Next, share some hunch you have about yourself that relates to that issue. Go "below the surface," as it were; get in touch with possible blind spots. Try to develop a new perspective on yourself and that issue, one that might help you see the issue more clearly so that you might begin to think of how you might act on it.
7.   In some way suggested by your instructor, share your examples with one or more members of your group and give one another feedback.

Example 1

A man, 25, in a counselor training group believes that his experience in the training group is giving him some second thoughts about his ability and willingness to get close to others.

Level-1 understanding: "I like people and I show this by my willingness to work hard with them. For instance, in this group I see myself as a hard worker. I listen to others carefully and I try to respond carefully. I see myself as a very active member of this group. I take the initiative in contacting others. I like working with the people here."

Level-2 understanding: "If I look closer at what I'm doing here, I realize that underneath my 'hardworking' and competent exterior, I am uncomfortable. I come to these sessions with more misgivings than I have admitted, even to myself. My hunch is that I have some fears about human closeness. I am afraid, both here and in a couple of relationships outside the group, that someone is going to ask me for more than I want to give. This keeps me on edge here. It keeps me on edge in a couple of relationships outside."

Now this trainee can talk to specific members of the group and discuss what he fears might be asked of him. This is a step toward handling his fear of closeness.

Example 2

A woman, 33, in a counselor training group, sees that her experience in the group is making her explore her attitude toward herself. It might not be as positive as she thought. She sees this as something that could interfere with her effectiveness as a counselor.

Level-1 understanding: "I like myself. I base this on the fact that I seem to relate freely to others. There are a number of things I like specifically about myself. I'm fairly bright. And I think I can use my intelligence to work with others as a helper. I work hard. I'm demanding of myself, but I don't place unreasonable demands on others."

Level-2 understanding: "If I look more closely at myself, I see that when I work hard it is because I feel I have to. My hunch is that 'I have to' counts more in my hard work than 'I want to.' I get pleasure out of working hard, but it also keeps me from feeling guilty. If I don't work 'hard enough,' then I can feel guilty or down on myself. I am beginning to feel that there is too much of the 'I must be a perfect person' in me. I judge myself <u>and</u> others more harshly than I care to think."

She goes on to explore the kinds of "sentences" she says to herself about herself and the ways in which she might be judging her fellow trainees.

1. First, choose three areas, issues, or concerns in your life around which you might develop the kinds of advanced empathic hunches illustrated in the examples. Just choose the areas without spelling out the hunches.

a. _____

_____

b. _____

_____

c. _____

_____

2. As in the examples, develop Level-1 (basic) and Level-2 (advanced empathy) hunches about yourself--your experiences, your behaviors, your feelings--in each area. Do this work on separate sheets of paper.
3. In a small group, choose one of the issues and share it with your fellow trainees. All the members of the group should use basic empathy and probes to help one another develop clarity.
4. Jot down a significant learning about yourself and the helping process in your journal.

EXERCISE 30: ADVANCED EMPATHY AND ACTION

The purpose of empathy is to help clients develop the kind of insight that will lead to problem-managing action. What you have learned about yourself in the previous exercise should serve as the basis of action in your own life.

1. Review the hunches you have developed about yourself in the three areas considered in the previous exercise.
2. In each problem or undeveloped-opportunity area ask yourself: "Given my new insights into these issues, what prudent actions could I take to manage the problem more effectively or develop the opportunity more aggressively?"
3. Write your responses on separate sheets of paper.
4. In a small group, share with your fellow trainees the work you have done in one of these areas.

Use empathy and probing to help one another clarify these actions more fully.
5. Using the criteria discussed earlier in this manual, give one another feedback on the actions outlined. Are there other actions that could be taken that manage the problem or develop the opportunity more fully?
6. Jot down any key learnings about yourself or the helping process in your journal.

In effective helping, insights serve the cause of problem-managing action. In ineffective helping, insights lead to further insights and the helping process loses the name of action.

EXERCISE 31: THE DISTINCTION BETWEEN BASIC AND ADVANCED EMPATHY

In this exercise, assume that the helper and the client have established a good working relationship, that the client's concerns have been explored from his or her perspective, and that the client needs to be challenged to see the problem situation from some new perspective or to act on the insights that have been developed.

1. In each instance, imagine the client speaking directly to you.
2. In (a) respond to what the client has just said with basic empathy. Use the formula or your own words.
3. Next, formulate one or two hunches about this person's experiences, behaviors, or feelings, hunches that, when shared, would help promote understanding and/or action. Use the material in the "context" section together with the client's words to formulate your hunches. Ask yourself: "On what clues am I basing this hunch?"
4. Then in (b) respond with some form of advanced empathy, that is, share some hunch that you believe will be useful for him or her. Share it in a way that will not put the client off.
5. Indicate the basis of your hunch.

Example

Context. A man, 48, husband and father, is exploring the poor relationships he has with his wife and children. In general, he feels that <u>he</u> is the victim, that his family is not treating him right (that is, like many clients, he emphasizes his experience rather than his behavior). He has not yet examined the implications of the ways he behaves toward his family. At this point he is talking about his sense of humor.

Client. "For instance, I get a lot of encouragement for being witty at parties. Almost everyone laughs. I think I provide a lot of entertainment, and others like it. But this is another way I seem to flop at home. When I try to be funny, my wife and kids don't laugh, at least not much. At times they even take my humor wrong and get angry. I actually have to watch my step in my own home."

a. **Basic empathy.** <u>"It's irritating when your own family doesn't seem to appreciate what you see as one of your talents."</u>
b. **Hunch.** <u>The family wants a husband and father, not a humorist. His humor, especially at home, is not as harmless as he thinks.</u>
c. **Advanced empathy.** <u>"I wonder whether their reaction to you could be interpreted differently. For instance, they might not want an entertainer at home, but just a husband and father. You know, just you."</u>
d. **Basis of hunch.** <u>His tendency to blame others; his inadequate exploration of the effects of his own behavior; common sense.</u>

1. **Context.** A first-year engineering graduate student has been exploring his disappointment with himself and with his performance in school. He has explored such issues as his dislike for the school and for some of the teachers with his counselor.

Client. "I just don't have much enthusiasm. My grades are just okay, maybe even a little

79

below par. I know I could do better if I wanted to. I don't know why my disappointment with the school and some of the faculty members can get to me so much. It's not like me. Ever since I can remember--even in primary school, when I didn't have any idea what an engineer was--I've wanted to be an engineer. Theoretically, I should be as happy as a lark because I'm in graduate school, but I'm not."

a. **Basic empathy.** _____

_____

_____

b. **Hunch.** _____

_____

_____

c. **Advanced empathy.** _____

_____

_____

_____

d. **Basis of a hunch** _____

_____

2. **Context.** This man, now 64, retired early from work when he was 62. He and his wife wanted to take full advantage of the years they had left. But his wife died a year after he retired. At the urging of friends he has finally come to a counselor. He has been exploring some of the problems his retirement has created for him. His two married sons live with their families in other cities. In the counseling sessions he has been dealing somewhat repetitiously with the theme of loss.

Client. "I seldom see the kids. I enjoy them and their families a lot when they do come. I get along real well with their wives. But now that my wife is gone . . . (pause) . . . and since I've stopped working . . . (pause) . . . I seem to just ramble around the house aimlessly, which is not like me at all. I suppose I should get rid of the house, but it's filled with a lot of memories--bittersweet memories now. There were a lot of good years here. The years seem to have slipped by and caught me unawares."

a. **Basic empathy.** _____

_____

_____

b. **Hunch.** _____

c. Advanced empathy._____

_____

_____

_____

d. Basis of hunch._____

_____

3. **Context.** A single woman, 33, is talking to a minister about the quality of her social life. She has a very close friend and she counts on her a great deal. She is exploring the ups and downs of this relationship. In the counseling sessions this woman comes on a bit loud and somewhat aggressive.

Client. "Ruth and I are on again off again with each other lately. When we're on, it's great. We have lunch together, go shopping, all that kind of stuff. But sometimes she seems to click off. You know, she tries to avoid me. But that's not easy to do. I keep after her. She's been pretty elusive for about two weeks now. I don't know why she runs away like this. I know we have our differences. She quieter and I'm the louder type. But our differences don't ordinarily seem to get in the way."

a. **Basic empathy.**_____

_____

_____

b. **Hunch.**_____

_____

_____

c. **Advanced empathy.**_____

_____

_____

d. **Basis of hunch.**_____

81

4. **Context.** A man, 40, is talking to a marriage counselor. This is the third time he has come to see the counselor over the past four years. His wife has never come with him. The other times he spent only a session or two with the counselor and then dropped out. In this session he has been talking a great deal about his latest annoyances with his wife.

Client. "I could go on telling you what she does and doesn't do. It's a litany. She really knows how to punish, not only me but others. I don't even know why I keep putting up with it. I want her to come to counseling, but she won't come. So, here I am again, in her place."

a. **Basic empathy.** _____

_____

_____

b. **Hunch.** _____

_____

_____

c. **Advanced empathy.** _____

_____

_____

d. **Basis of hunch.** _____

_____

5. **Context.** A high-school senior is talking to a school counselor about college and what kinds of courses she might take there. However, she also mentions, somewhat tentatively, her disappointment in not being chosen as valedictorian of her class. She and almost everyone else had expected her to be chosen.

Client. "I know that I would have liked to have been the class valedictorian, but I'm not so sure that you are supposed to count on anything like that. They chose Jane. She'll be good. She speaks well and she's very popular. But no one has a <u>right</u> to be valedictorian. I'd be kidding myself if I thought differently. I've done better in school than Jane, but I'm not as outgoing or popular."

a. **Basic empathy.** _____

_____

b. **Hunch.**_____

_____

_____

c. **Advanced empathy.**_____

_____

_____

_____

d. **Basis of hunch.**_____

_____

6. **Context.** A college professor, 43, is talking to a friend, who happens to be a counselor, about his values. He is vaguely dissatisfied with his priorities, but has never done much about examining his current values in any serious way. From time to time the two of them talk about values, but no conclusions are reached. He is not married. Work seems to be a primary value.

Client. "Well, it's no news to you that I work a lot. There's literally no day I get up and say to myself, 'Well, today is a day off and I can just do what I want.' It sounds terrible when I put it that way. I've been going on like that for about ten years now. It seems that I should do something about it. But it's obviously my choice. I'm doing what I doing freely. No one's got a gun to my head."

a. **Basic empathy.**_____

_____

_____

b. **Hunch.**_____

_____

_____

c. **Advanced empathy.**_____

_____

_____

d. **Basis of hunch.**_____

_____

7. **Context.** A man, 50, with a variety of problems in living is talking with a counselor. His tendency has been to ruminate almost constantly on his defects. He begins a second interview on this somewhat sour note.

Client. "To make myself feel bad, all I have to do is review what has happened to me in the past and take a good look at what is happening to me right now. This past year, I let my drinking problem get the best of me for four months. Over the years, I done lots of things to mess up my marriage. For instance, like changing jobs all the time. Now my wife and I are separated. I don't earn enough money to give her much, and the thought of getting another job is silly with the economy the way it is. I'm not so sure what skills I have to market, anyway."

a. **Basic empathy.**_____

_____

_____

b. **Hunch.**_____

_____

_____

c. **Advanced empathy.**_____

_____

_____

_____

d. **Basis of hunch.**_____

_____

8. **Context.** A divorced woman, 35, with a daughter, 12, is talking to a counselor about her current relationship with men. She mentions that she has lied to her daughter about her sex life. She has told her that she doesn't have sexual relations with men, but she does. In general she seems quite protective of her daughter. From what her mother says, however, the young girl does not seem to have any serious problems.

Client. "I don't want to hurt my daughter by letting her see my shadow side. I don't know whether she could handle it. What do you think? I'd like to be honest and tell her everything. I just don't want her to think less of me. I like sex. I've been used to it in marriage, and it's just too hard to give it up. I wish you could tell me what to do about my daughter."

a. **Basic empathy.**

_____

_____

_____

b. **Hunch.**

_____

_____

_____

c. **Advanced empathy.**

_____

_____

_____

_____

d. **Basis of hunch.**

_____

_____

9. **Context.** The wife of this man, 35, has recently left him. He tried desperately to get her back, but she wanted a divorce. As part of his strategy to get her back he examined his role in the marriage and freely "confessed" to both the counselor and his wife what he felt he was doing wrong in the relationship. Part of his problem in his relationships with both his wife and others was a need to get the better of her and others in arguments. He could never admit that he might have been wrong.

    Client. "I don't know what's wrong with her. I've given her everything she wanted. I mean I've admitted all my mistakes. I was even willing to take the blame for things that I thought were her fault. But she's not interested in a reformed me! Damned if you do, damned if you don't."

a. **Basic empathy.**

_____

_____

_____

b. **Hunch.**

_____

_____

_____

c. **Advanced empathy.**

_____

_____

_____

_____

d. **Basis of hunch.**_____

_____

10. **Context.** A nun, 44, a member of a counselor training group, has been talking about her dissatisfaction with her present job. Although a nurse, she is presently teaching in a primary school because, she says, of the "urgent needs" of that school. When pressed, she refers briefly to a history of job dissatisfaction. In the group she has shown herself to be an active, intelligent, and caring woman who tends to speak and act in self-effacing ways. She mentions how obedience has been stressed throughout her years in the religious order. She does mention, however, that things have been "letting up a bit" in recent years. The younger sisters don't seem to be as preoccupied with obedience as she is.

   Client. "The reason I'm talking about my job is that I don't want to become a counselor and then discover it's another job I'm dissatisfied with. It would be unfair to the people I'd be working with and unfair to my religious order, which is paying for my education. Of course, I have no iron-clad assurance that I'll be put in a job that will enable me to use my counselor training."

a. **Basic empathy.**_____

_____

_____

b. **Hunch.**_____

_____

_____

c. **Advanced empathy.**_____

_____

_____

_____

d. **Basis of hunch.**_____

_____

HELPER SELF-DISCLOSURE

Although helpers should be **ready** to make disclosures about themselves that would help their clients understand their problem situations more clearly, they should do so only if such disclosures do not upset their clients or distract their clients from the work they are doing. Read the text on helper self-disclosure before doing this exercise.

EXERCISE 32: EXPERIENCES OF MINE THAT MIGHT BE HELPFUL TO OTHERS

In this exercise you are asked to review some problems in living that you feel you have managed or are managing successfully. Indicate what you might share about yourself that would help a client with a similar problem situation understand that problem situation or some part of it more clearly and move on to problem-managing action. That is, what might you share of yourself that would help the client move forward in the problem-managing process?

Example 1

Trainee. "In the past I have been an expert in feeling sorry for myself whenever I had to face any kind of difficulty. I know very well the rewards of seeing myself as victim. I used to fantasize myself as victim as a form of daydreaming or recreation. I think many clients get mired down in their problems because they let themselves feel sorry for themselves the way I did. I think I can spot this tendency in others. When I see this happening, I think I could share brief examples from my own experience and then ask clients to see if what I was doing squares with what they see themselves doing now."

Example 2

Trainee. "I have been addicted to a number of things in my life and I see a common pattern in different kinds of addiction. For instance, I have been addicted to alcohol, to cigarettes, and to sleeping pills. I have also been addicted to people. By this I mean that at times in my life I have been a very dependent person and I found the same kind of symptoms in dependency that I did in addiction. I know a lot about the fear of letting go and the pain of withdrawal. I think I could share some of this in ways that would not accuse or frighten clients or distract them from their own concerns."

1. List four areas in which you feel you have something to share that might help clients who have problems in living similar to your own. Just briefly indicate the area.

a. _____

b. _____

c. _____

d. _____

2. On separate paper make more extended comments in each area, comments similar to those in the examples.
3. Share one or two with your fellow trainees. Give and get feedback on the usefulness of the disclosures.

EXERCISE 33: APPROPRIATENESS OF HELPER SELF-DISCLOSURE

In this exercise you are asked to review the client situations presented in Exercise 31. In each case, ask yourself if you feel that sharing your own experience might in some way help the client. Note that this does not mean that you would necessarily share your experience. You are being asked only to see if you have some experience that might help the client see his or her problem more clearly. Consider the following example (which is also the example used in Exercise 31).

Context. A man, 48, husband and father, is exploring the poor relationships he has with his wife and children. In general he feels that he is the victim. He feels that his family is not treating him right, that is, like many clients, he emphasizes what others are doing to him rather than his own behavior. He has not yet examined the implications of the ways he behaves toward his family. At this point he is talking about his sense of humor.

Client. "For instance, I get a lot of encouragement for being witty at parties. Almost everyone laughs. I think I provide a lot of entertainment, and others like it. But this is another way I seem to flop at home. When I try to be funny, my wife and kids don't laugh, at least not much. At times they even take my humor wrong and get angry. I actually have to watch my step in my own home."

First of all, assume that you respond with basic, accurate empathy, as in Exercise 31. Then ask yourself whether you have any experience that might help the client see the problem situation more clearly. If so, mention what this experience is.

My experience. "A person who was trying to become close to me once told me that he found it difficult to get past my humor and make contact with me. I was startled and began to see how I was using humor to keep people at a distance. In my case, it was one way I controlled what happened in relationships."

Now review each case in Exercise 31 and see whether you have some personal experience that might help the client get a better grasp of his or her problem. On separate paper jot down what you think could be helpful if presented in the right way.

EXERCISE 34: PRACTICING SELF-SHARING IN COUNSELING INTERVIEWS

In this exercise, you are asked to try your hand at sharing your experience to help your client see his or her problem situation more clearly.

1. The training group should be divided into groups of three -- helper, client, and observer.
2. The client should continue to discuss a problem situation with which the helper is familiar, that is, one that has already been explored to some degree.
3. Spend between five and ten minutes in a helping session. If you are the helper, once or twice during the session try to share an experience of yours that you think might help the client. Be brief

and focused. Present your experience in such a way as not to distract the client from his or her own concerns.

4.   When time is up, the observer and client give the helper feedback on the usefulness of the disclosure.

* How pertinent was it?
* How brief and focused was it?
* To what degree were the client's concerns kept front and center?
* What use did the client make of the helper's disclosure?
* How challenging was the disclosure?

5.   Repeat this exercise until each member of the three-person group has had the opportunity to be the helper.

6.   Debrief the exercise in the total training group. Deal with the following question: What is the overall place of helper self-sharing in the helping process? What are the advantages? What are the disadvantages?

CHALLENGING DISCREPANCIES

Challenging is a skill in which you invite clients to examine discrepancies that they are perhaps overlooking and that keep them locked into problem situations. Furthermore, challenges should be descriptions rather than accusations. If they sound like accusations rather than invitations, they tend to elicit defensive reactions in clients.

EXERCISE 35:   CHALLENGING ONE'S OWN STRENGTHS

One of the best forms of challenge is to invite clients to examine unused strengths and resources that could be used to manage some problem situation more effectively. In this exercise you are asked to confront yourself with respect to your own unused or underused strengths and resources. The discrepancy is that you have a resource but do not use it effectively.

Example

Problem Situation. "My social life is not nearly as full as I would like it to be."

Description of unused strengths or resources. "I have problem-solving skills, but I don't apply them to the practical problems of everyday life such as my less than adequate social life. Instead of defining goals for myself (making acquaintances, developing friendships) and then seeing how many different ways I could go about achieving these goals, I wait around to see if something will happen to make my social life fuller. I remain passive even though I have the skills to become active."

Now consider three problem situations or parts of problem situations you have been working on.

1.   Briefly identify the problem situation.
2.   Describe the problem situation or some part of it in terms of some strength, ability, or resource you are not using or are not using as fully as you might.

1. **Problem situation.**_____

_____

_____

Underused strengths._____

_____

_____

_____

_____

2. Problem situation._____

_____

Underused strengths._____

_____

_____

_____

_____

3. Problem situation._____

_____

Underused strengths._____

_____

_____

_____

_____

EXERCISE 36: CHALLENGING DISCREPANCIES IN ONE'S OWN LIFE

Most of us face a variety of self-defeating discrepancies in our lives besides the discrepancies that involve unused strengths and resources. We all allow ourselves, to a greater or lesser extent, to becomes victims of our own prejudices, smokescreens, distortions, and self-deceptions. In this exercise you are asked to confront some of these, especially the kind of discrepancies that might affect the quality of your helping or the quality of your membership in the training group.

Example 1

The issue. "I am very controlling in my relationships with others."

The description. "I am very controlling in my relationships with others. For instance, in social situations I manipulate people into doing what I want to do. I do this as subtly as possible. I find out what everyone wants to do and then I use one against the other and gentle persuasion to steer people in the direction in which I want to go. In the training sessions I try to get people to talk about problems that are of interest to me. I even use empathy and probes to steer people in directions I might find interesting. All this is so much a part of my style that usually I don't even notice it. I see this as selfish, but yet I experience little guilt about it."

Example 2

The issue. This trainee confronts her need for approval from others.

The description. "Most people see me as a 'nice' person. Part of this I like, part of it is a smokescreen. Being nice is my best defense against harshness and criticism from others. I'm cooperative. I compliment others easily. I'm not cynical or sarcastic. I've gotten to enjoy this kind of being 'nice.' I find it rewarding. But it also means that I seldom talk about ideas that might offend others. My feedback to others in the group is almost always positive. I let others give feedback on mistakes. Outside the group I steer clear of controversial conversations. But I'm beginning to feel very bland."

Now confront yourself in three areas that, if dealt with, will help you be a more effective trainee and helper. In the description section be as specific as you can. Describe specific experiences, behaviors, feelings. Give brief examples.

1. **The issue.**_____

_____

Descriptive self-challenge._____

_____

_____

_____

_____

_____

_____

_____

_____

2. The issue _____

_____

Descriptive self-challenge _____

_____

_____

_____

_____

_____

_____

_____

_____

3. The issue _____

_____

Descriptive self-challenge _____

_____

_____

_____

_____

_____

_____

_____

_____

EXERCISE 37: THE CHALLENGE ROUND ROBIN

The purpose of this exercise is to give you the opportunity to practice both challenging others and responding non-defensively and creatively to those who challenge you. The assumption is that you have begun to know the other members of your training group fairly well and that you are thoroughly familiar with the principles and methodology of effective challenging.

1.   Review the material on challenging and effective response to challenge in Chapters Eight and Nine of the text.
2.   Divide up into groups of three. The three roles are challenger, person being challenged, and observer. Challengers will do two things: (a) point out something they have noticed that their partners do well in the training group and then (b) challenge their partners in some way (for instance, by pointing out a strength or resource that is being underused or some other discrepancy, being careful to be descriptive rather than accusatory).
3.   The person being challenged first responds with basic empathy to make sure that he or she understands the point of the challenge.
4.   Then the partners briefly explore the area challenged in terms of concrete experiences, behaviors, and feelings.
5.   Afterward, the observer gives feedback both to the challenger in terms of style, specificity, and usefulness of the challenge and to the person being challenged in terms of effective collaboration in the challenging process.
6.   Each person in the triad is given a chance to play all three roles.

Example

Challenger. "In our group sessions, you take pains to see to it that other members of the group are understood, especially when they talk about sensitive issues. You provide a great deal of empathy and you encourage others, principally by your example, to do the same. Your empathy never sounds phony and most of the time you're quite accurate.

However, you tend to limit yourself to basic empathy. You seldom use probes and you seem to be slow to challenge anyone, for instance, by sharing hunches that would help others see their interactional styles more clearly. Because of your empathy and your genuineness, you have amassed a lot of 'credits' in the group, but you don't use them to help others make reasonable demands on themselves."

Person challenged. "You appreciate my ability and willingness to be empathic. But I am less effective than I might be in that I don't move beyond empathy, especially since I 'merit' doing so. I should work on increasing my challenging skills."

A and B then spend a few minutes exploring the issue that has been raised.

IMMEDIACY: EXPLORING RELATIONSHIPS

As noted in the text, your ability to deal directly with what is happening between you and your clients in the helping sessions themselves is an important skill. **Relationship** immediacy refers to your ability to review the history and present status of your relationship with other members of your group--who are both your fellow trainees and your "clients"--in concrete behavioral ways. **Here-and-now** immediacy refers to your ability to deal with a particular situation that is affecting the ways in which you and another person are relating right now, in this moment.

Immediacy is a complex skill. It involves (1) revealing how you are being affected by the other person, (2) exploring your own behavior toward the other person, (3) sharing hunches about his or her behavior toward you or pointing out discrepancies, distortions, smokescreens, and the like, and (4) inviting the other person to explore the relationship with a view to developing a better working relationship. For instance, if you see that a client is manifesting hostility toward you in subtle, hard-to-get-at ways, you may   (1) let the client know how you are being affected by what is happening in the relationship (that is, you share your experience), (2) explore how you might be contributing to the difficulty, (3) describe the client's behavior and share reasonable hunches about what is happening (challenge), and (4) invite the client to examine in a direct way what is happening in the relationship. Immediacy involves collaborative problem solving with respect to the relationship itself.

EXERCISE 38: IMMEDIACY IN YOUR INTERPERSONAL LIFE

In this exercise you are asked to review some issues that remain "unfinished" between you and others <u>outside</u> the training group.

1.   Think of people in your life with whom you have some unresolved or undealt-with "you-me" issues (relatives, friends, intimates, co-workers, and so forth).
2.   Briefly indicate what the issue is.
3.   Imagine yourself talking with one of these individuals face to face.
4.   Be immediate with this person with a view to instituting the kind of dialogue that would help the two of you grapple with the issue that concerns you. Your immediacy statement should include (a) the issue and how it is affecting you, (b) some indication of how you might be contributing to the difficulty, (c) some kind of concrete challenge, and (d) an invitation to the other person to engage in dialogue with you on this issue.
5.   Remember that initial challenges should be appropriately tentative.

Example 1

The issue. A trainee sees herself speaking to a friend outside the group. She is dissatisfied with the depth of sharing in the relationship. She is hesitant about revealing her own deeper thoughts, values, and concerns.

Trainee talking directly to her friend. "I'm a bit embarrassed about what I'm going to say. I think we enjoy being with each other. But I feel some reluctance in talking to you about some of my deeper thoughts and concerns. And, if I'm not mistaken, I see some of the same kind of reluctance in you. For instance, the other day both of us seemed to be pretty awkward when we talked a bit about religion. We dropped the subject pretty quickly. I'm embarrassed right now because I feel that I may be violating the 'not-too-deep' rule that we've perhaps stumbled into. I'm wondering what you might think about all this."

Example 2

The issue. A trainee is speaking about her relationship with her boss. She feels that he respects her but, because she is a woman, he does not think of her as a prospect for managerial training.

The trainee, talking to her boss. "I think you see me as a good worker. As far as I can tell, you and I work well together. Even though you're my boss, I see a sort of equality between us. I mean that you don't push your boss role. And yet something bothers me. Every now and then I pick up clues that you don't think of me when you're considering people for managerial training slots. You seem to be very satisfied with my work, but part of that seems to be being satisfied with keeping me in the slot I'm in. I don't see you as offensively sexist at all, but something tells me that you might unconsciously think of men for training slots before women. Maybe it's part of the culture here. It would be helpful for me if we could explore this a bit."

Now write out three statements of immediacy dealing with people in your life outside the training group. Choose people and issues that you would be willing to discuss in the group. Obviously you need not reveal the identity of the people involved.

1. **The issue.**_____

_____

_____

_____

Write out a face-to-face statement on separate paper.

2. **The issue.**_____

_____

_____

_____

Write out a face-to-face statement on separate paper.

3. **The issue.**_____

_____

_____

_____

Write out a face-to-face statement on separate paper.

EXERCISE 39: RESPONDING TO SITUATIONS CALLING FOR IMMEDIACY

In this exercise a number of client-helper situations calling for some kind of immediacy on your part are described. You are asked to consider each situation and respond with some statement of immediacy. Consider the following example.

Example

Situation. This client, a man of 44, occasionally makes snide remarks either about the helping profession itself or some of the things that you do in your interactions with him. At times he is cooperative, but at times he asks you to make decisions for him. "Just tell me the best way for me to tell my boss that he's an idiot." He makes remarks about you personally at times, "I bet you've got a lot of friends." Or, on being confronted by you, "I hope you're a little more caring with the people in your 'real' world."

Immediacy response. "Tom, let's stop a minute and explore what's happening between you and me in our sessions. . . . (Tom says, "Oh, oh, here we go!") . . . You take mild swipes at the counseling profession such as, 'I hear people are still trying to find out whether counseling works.' Or at me like, 'Oh, oh, Mr. Counselor is getting a little hot under the collar.' I've ignored these remarks, but in ignoring them I've become a kind of accomplice in your behavior. Sometimes we seem to be working like a team. Other times you ask me to make decisions for you, you know, the 'Just Tell Me' routine. I've let myself get on edge with you and that's not helping us at all. . . . (Tom says, "You want to call my games, huh?") . . . Tom, I don't want to play games. Not with myself, you, or any of my clients. Let's re-do the relationship part of our contract."

Now consider the following situations and write out an immediacy response that challenges the client's perspectives and/or actions.

1. **The situation.** The client is a person of the opposite sex. You have had several sessions with this person. It has become evident that the person is attracted to you and has begun to make thinly disguised overtures for more intimacy. The person finds you both socially and sexually attractive. Some of the overtures have sexual overtones.

Immediacy response.

_____

_____

_____

_____

_____

_____

_____

_____

2. **The situation.** In the first session you and the client, a relatively successful businessman, 40, have discussed the issue of fees. At that time you mentioned that it is difficult for you to talk about money, but you finally settled on a fee at the modest end of the going rates. He told you that he thought that the fee was "more than fair." However, during the next few sessions he drops hints about how expensive this venture is proving to be. He talks about getting finished as quickly as possible and intimates that that is your responsibility. You, who thought that the money issue had been resolved, find it still very much alive.

Immediacy response.

_____

_____

_____

_____

_____

_____

_____

3. **The situation.** The client is a male, 22, who is obliged to see you as part of being put on probation for a crime he committed. He is cooperative for a session or two and then becomes quite resistant. His resistance takes the form of both subtle and not too subtle questioning of your competence, questioning the value of this kind of helping, coming late for sessions, and generally treating you like an unnecessary burden.

Immediacy response._____

_____

_____

_____

_____

_____

_____

_____

4. **The situation.** You are a woman. The client, 19, reminds you of your own son, 17, toward whom you have mixed feelings as he struggles to establish some kind of reasonable independence from you. The client at times acts in very dependent ways toward you, telling you that he is glad that you are helping him, asking your advice, and in various ways taking a "little boy" posture toward you. At other times he seems to wish that he didn't have anything to do with you at all and accuses you of being "like his mother."

Immediacy response._____

_____

_____

_____

_____

_____

_____

_____

EXERCISE 40: IMMEDIACY WITH THE OTHER MEMBERS OF YOUR TRAINING GROUP

1.   Review the general directions for Exercise 38.

2. Read the example below.

3. On separate paper, write out a statement of immediacy for the members of your training group (or selected members if the group is large). Imagine yourself in a face-to-face situation with each member successively. Deal with real issues that pertain to the training sessions, interactional style, and so forth.

4. In a round robin, share with each of the other members of the group the statement you have written for him or her.

5. The person listening to the immediacy statement should reply with empathy, making sure that he or she has heard the statement correctly.

6. Listen to the immediacy statement the other person has for you and then reply with empathy.

7. Finally, discuss for <u>a few minutes</u> the quality of your relationship with each other in the training group.

8. Continue with the round robin until each person has had the opportunity to share an immediacy statement with every other member.

Example

Trainee A to Trainee B. "I notice that you and I have relatively little interaction in the group. You give me little feedback; I give you little feedback. It's almost as if there is some kind of conspiracy of non-interaction between us. I like you and the way you act in the group. For instance, I like the way you challenge others, carefully but without any apology. I think I refrain from giving you feedback, at least negative feedback, because I don't want to alienate you. I do little to make contact with you. I have a hunch that you'd like to talk to me more than you do, but it's just a hunch. I'd like to hear your side of our story, or non-story, as the case might be."

Identify the elements of immediacy (self-disclosure, challenge, invitation) in this example. Then move on to the exercise.

STEP I-C: LEVERAGE: WORKING ON ISSUES THAT MAKE A DIFFERENCE

The exercises in this section deal with two tasks: helping clients work on issues that will make a difference in their lives, that is, issues that have "leverage," and helping them "focus" on the kind of detail that can help them understand and deal with the issues chosen for exploration.

LEVERAGE: CHOOSING ISSUES THAT COUNT

Clients may need help in determining whether their issues are important enough to bring to a helper in the first place. This is called "screening."

EXERCISE 41: SCREENING

1. Read these two case summaries with a view to discussing them with your fellow trainees.

Case 1

Lila comes to a counselor for help. In telling her story, she says that she has occasional headaches and a few arguments with her husband, Lance. Doctors have told her that there is nothing wrong with her physically. The helper, using empathy, probing, and an occasional challenge, discovers that Lila is not understating the nature of her concerns and that there are no further hidden issues. She does discover that Lila and Lance have no children, that Lance works rather long hours in his new job, and that Lila is mainly a householder in their small condominium and has few outside interests.

98

Case 2

Ray, 41, is a middle manager in a manufacturing company located in a large city. He goes to see a counselor with a somewhat complex story. He is bored with his job; his marriage is lifeless; he has poor rapport with his two teenage children, one of whom is having trouble with drugs; he is drinking heavily; his self-esteem is low; he has begun to steal things, small things, not because he needs them but because he gets a kick out of it. He tells his story in a rather disjointed way, skipping around from one problem area to another. He is a talented, personable, engaging man who seems to be adrift in life. He does not show any symptoms of severe psychiatric illness. He does experience a great deal of unease in talking about himself. This is his first visit to a helper.

2. Discuss these two cases in terms of the material in the text on screening. How would you approach the woman in Case 1? Under what conditions would you be willing to work with her? How would you approach the man in Case 2? In what general ways does this case differ from Case 1? What would your concerns be in working with the man in Case 2?

EXERCISE 42: CHOOSING ISSUES THAT MAKE A DIFFERENCE

Often enough, the stories clients tell are quite complex. And so they may need your help in deciding which issues to work on first and which merit substantial attention.

In this exercise you are asked to review the personal concerns and problems you have identified in doing the exercises in this manual, especially the exercises in Step I-A.

1. Briefly list as many of the concerns or unexploited opportunities you have discovered in doing the assessment exercises as you can recall.

_____

_____

_____

_____

_____

_____

_____

_____

_____

_____

_____

_____

2. First, do some screening. Put a line through those that you would probably not bring to a counselor because they are not that important or because you believe that you could handle them easily if you wanted to.
3. Next, using the criteria below, evaluate the items remaining on your list. Next to each concern place the letters of the applicable "leverage" criteria listed below.

Example

Gino is a trainee in a clinical psychology program. Here is one of the concerns on his list:

* "I am very inconsistent in the way I deal with people. For instance, some of my friends see me as fickle, I blow hot and cold. One friend told me that whenever he sees me, he's not sure which Gino he will meet. In fact, I seem to be inconsistent in other areas of life. Sometimes I give myself wholeheartedly to my studies, sometimes I couldn't care less."

Gino believes that the following criteria apply: b, d, g, i.

a. **Crisis.** If there is a crisis, first help the client defuse and manage the crisis.
b. **Importance to client.** Begin with issues that the client sees as important.
c. **Distress.** Begin with a problem that seems to be causing significant distress for the client.
d. **Motivation.** Focus on issues, however important, that the client is willing to work on.
e. **Sub-problem.** Begin with some part or sub-problem of a larger problem situation.
f. **Manageability.** Begin with a problem that can be managed relatively easily, one that shows promise of being successfully handled by the client.
g. **Spread effect.** Begin with a problem that, if handled, will lead to some kind of general improvement in the client's overall condition.
h. **From the less to the more.** When it seems appropriate, move from less severe to more severe problems.
i. **Cost effectiveness.** Focus on a problem for which the benefits (outcomes) will outweigh the costs of the work needed to manage it.

4. Choose two or three issues that have high-leverage value for you. These are issues, concerns, opportunities, or problems, that, if pursued, would make a difference in your life.
5. In a small group, share one or two of these issues. Discuss what it would take to get you to invest time and energy in developing these opportunities or managing these problems.

FOCUSING: HELPING CLIENTS GET TO THE CORES OF PROBLEMS

It is not enough to help clients choose problems, issues, or concerns that make a difference. Once a problem situation is chosen, the issues within it need to be identified. If Connie and Chuck want to deal with the poor communication they have with each other in their marriage, then the key issues relating to communication or the lack thereof need to be identified and explored. You do this by using empathy, probing, and challenge to achieve the kind of problem clarity that can lead to goal setting and strategy formulation.

A problem or unused opportunity is clear if it is spelled out in terms of specific experiences, specific behaviors, and specific feelings in specific situations.

EXERCISE 43: SPEAKING CONCRETELY ABOUT EXPERIENCES

Clients often speak too vaguely about their problems. Helpers often go "'round the mulberry bush" with them, allowing them to be too general. Vague problems lead only to vague solutions. Vague solutions are worthless. Since problem situations are spelled out in terms of experiences, behaviors, and feelings, we start with experiences, your experiences. In this exercise, you are asked to speak of some of your experiences, first vaguely, then concretely.

Example 1

* **Vague statement of experience.** "I'm sometimes less efficient than I could be because of headaches."
* **Concrete statement of the same experience.** "I get migraine headaches about once a week. They make me extremely sensitive to light and usually cause severe pain. I often get so sick that I throw up. They happen more often when I'm tense or under a lot of pressure. For instance, I often come away from a visit with my ex-wife with one. Each week they rob me of productive hours of work, either at work or at home."

Example 2

* **Vague statement of experience.** "My marriage is disintegrating."
* **Concrete statement of the same experience.** "My husband is going around with other women, though he won't admit it. He never asks me to have sex though occasionally it 'happens.' He is verbally abusive at times, though he has never hit me."

1. In the spaces below, explore three experiences, things you see as happening <u>to</u> you, that are related to some problem situation or situations of your own. Choose issues that might affect the quality of your helping.

a. **Vague.** _____

_____

Concrete. _____

_____

_____

_____

b. **Vague.** _____

_____

Concrete. _____

_____

_____

_____

c. **Vague.** _____

_____

Concrete. _____

2. Share one or two of these with the members of a small group. Get feedback on how clear your second statement is. If you do not think that someone's statement is as clear as it might be, use probes and challenges to help your fellow trainee make his or her statement clearer.

EXERCISE 44: SPEAKING CONCRETELY ABOUT YOUR BEHAVIOR

In this exercise, you are asked to speak about some of your behaviors (what you do or fail to do) that are involved in some problem situation. As in the exercise above, start with a vague statement, then clarify it with the kind of detail needed to serve the problem-management process. Choose a problem situation that might affect you in your role as helper.

Example 1

* **Vague statement of behavior.** "I tend to be domineering."
* **Concrete statement of the same behavior.** "I try, usually in subtle ways, to get others to do what I want to do. I even pride myself on this. In conversations, I take the lead. I interrupt others, jokingly and in a good-natured way, but I make my points. If a friend is talking about something serious when I'm not in the mood to hear it, I change the subject."

Example 2

* **Vague statement of behavior.** "I don't treat my wife right."
* **Concrete statement of the same behavior.** "When I come home from work, I read the paper and watch some TV. I don't talk much to my wife except a bit at supper. I don't share the little things that went on in my day. Neither do I encourage her to talk about what happened to her. Still, if I feel like having sex later, I expect her to hop in bed with me willingly."

1. In the spaces below, deal with three instances of your own behavior. Stick to describing what you do or fail to do rather than experiences or feelings. Choose situations and behaviors that are relevant to your role as helper.

a. **Vague.** _____

_____

Concrete. _____

_____

_____

_____

_____

b. **Vague.** _____

_____

    Concrete. _____

_____

_____

_____

_____

c. **Vague.** _____

_____

    Concrete. _____

_____

_____

_____

_____

2. Share one or two of these with the members of a small group. Get feedback on how clear your second statement is. If you do not think that someone's statement is as clear as it might be, use probes and challenges to help your fellow trainee make his or her statement clearer.

EXERCISE 45:   SPEAKING CONCRETELY ABOUT FEELINGS AND EMOTIONS

       Feelings and emotions arise from experiences and behaviors. Therefore, it is unrealistic to talk about feelings without relating them to experiences or behaviors. However, in this exercise try to emphasize the feelings. Read the following examples.

Example 1

* **Vague statement of feelings.** "I get bothered in training groups."
* **Concrete statement of the same feelings.** "I feel hesitant and embarrassed whenever I want to give feedback to other trainees, especially if it is in any way negative. When the time comes, my heart

beats faster and my palms sweat. I feel like everyone is staring at me."

Example 2

* **Vague statement of feelings.** "I feel unsettled at times with my mother."
* **Concrete statement of the same feelings.** "I feel guilty and depressed whenever my mother calls and implies that she's lonely. I then get angry with myself for giving in to guilt so easily. Then the whole day has a pall over it. I get nervous and irritable and show it to others."

1. In the spaces below, deal with three instances of your own feelings. Try to focus on feelings that you have some trouble managing and that could interfere with your role as helper.

a. **Vague.** _____

_____

Concrete. _____

_____

_____

_____

_____

b. **Vague.** _____

_____

Concrete. _____

_____

_____

_____

c. **Vague.** _____

_____

Concrete. _____

_____

_____

2. Share one or two of these with the members of a small group. Get feedback on how clear your second statement is. If you do not think that someone's statement is as clear as it might be, use probes and challenges to help your fellow trainee make his or her statement clearer.

EXERCISE 46: SPEAKING CONCRETELY ABOUT EXPERIENCES, BEHAVIORS, FEELINGS

In this exercise, you are asked to bring together all three elements--specific experiences, specific behaviors, and specific feelings--in talking about some high-leverage personal concerns. Study the following examples.

Example

* **Vague statement.** "Sometimes I'm a rather overly sensitive and spiteful person."
* **Concrete statement.** "I do not take criticism well. When I receive almost any kind of negative feedback, I usually smile and seem to shrug it off, but inside I begin to pout. Also, deep inside, I put the person who gave me the feedback on a 'list.' I say to myself that that person is going to pay for what he or she did. I find this hard to admit, even to myself. It sounds so petty. For instance, two weeks ago in the training group I received some negative feedback from you, Cindy. I felt angry and hurt because I thought you were my 'friend.' Since then I've tried to see what mistakes you make here. I've been looking for an opportunity to get back at you. I've even felt bad because I haven't been able to catch you. I'm embarrassed to say all this."

Pick out the experiences, behaviors, and feelings in this example. Discuss to what degree the detail offered gets at the core of the problem situation. What probes would you use to help this person become even more specific?

1. Talk about two situations in terms of your own specific experiences, behaviors, and feelings. Deal with high-leverage themes that relate to your potential effectiveness as a helper. Choose detail that gets at the core of the problem or unused opportunity.

a. **Vague.** _____

_____

Concrete. _____

_____

_____

_____

_____

_____

_____

_____

_____

b. **Vague.** _____

_____

Concrete. _____

_____

_____

_____

_____

_____

_____

_____

_____

_____

_____

2. In a small group share and critique one of your high-leverage concerns. To what degree did the detail get at the core of the issue?

EXERCISE 47: COUNSELING YOURSELF: AN EXERCISE IN STAGE I

In this exercise you are asked to carry on a dialogue with yourself in writing.

Choose a problematic area of your life, one that is relevant to to your competence as a helper. First use empathy, probes, and challenges to help yourself tell your story. Choose a high-leverage issue for exploration. Work at clarifying it in terms of specific experiences, behaviors, and feelings. The dialogue should include probes for and challenges to problem-managing action.

Example

This example comes from the experience of Cormack, a man in a master's degree program in counseling psychology.

His Story. "To be frank, I have a number of misgivings about becoming a counselor. A number of things are turning me off. For instance, one of my instructors this past semester was an

106

arrogant guy. I kept saying to myself, 'Is this what these psychology programs produce? Could this guy really help anyone?' I also find the program much too theoretical. In a 'Theories of Counseling and Psychotherapy' course we never did anything, not even discuss the practical implications of these theories. And so they remained just that--theories. I'm very disappointed. I'm about to go into my second year, but I've got serious reservations. From what others tell me, the program gets a bit more practical, but not enough. There's a practicum experience at the end of the program, but I need more hands-on work now. So I've started working at a halfway house for people discharged from mental hospitals. But that's not working out the way I expected either. There's something about this whole helping business that is making me think twice about myself and about the profession."

Response to self. "All of this adds up to the fact that the helping profession, at least from your experience, is not what it's cracked up to be. The program and some of the instructors in it have left you disappointed. What do you find especially difficult to take?"

Self. "It's hard to say, but I think the halfway house bothers me most. Because that's not theoretical stuff. That's real stuff out there."

Response to self. "That's a place where real helping should be taking place. But you've got misgivings about what's going on there."

Self. "Yes, two sets of misgivings. One set about me and one about the place."

Response to self. "Which set do you want to explore?"

Self. "I feel I have to explore both, but I'll start with myself. I feel so ill-prepared. What's in the lectures and books seems so distant from the realities of the halfway house. For instance, the other day one of the residents there began yelling at me when we were passing in the hallway. She hit me a few times and then ran off screaming that I was after her."

Response to self. "It sounds frightening, upsetting. I'm wondering whether the more practical part of the counseling program you're going into would better prepare you for that kind of reality."

Self. "It could be. I may be doing myself in by jumping ahead of myself."

Response to self. "But you still have reservations about the effectiveness of the halfway house."

Self. "I wasn't ready for what I found there. I've been there a couple of months. No one has really helped me learn the ropes. I don't have an official supervisor. I see all sorts of people with problems and help when I can."

Response to self. "You just don't feel prepared and they don't do much to help you. So you feel inadequate. You also seem to be basing your judgments about the adequacy of helper-training programs and helping facilities on this training program and on the halfway house."

Self. "That's a good point. I'm making the assumption that both should be high-quality places. As far as I can tell, they're not. I guess I have to work on myself first. But that's why I went to the halfway house in the first place. I'm an independent person, but I'm too much on my own there. In a sense, I'm trusted but, since I don't get much supervision, I have to go on my own instincts and I'm not sure they're always right."

Response to self. "There's some comfort in being trusted, but without supervision you still have a what-am-I-doing-here feeling."

Self. "There are many times when I ask myself just that, 'What are you doing here?' I provide day-to-day services for a lot of people. I listen to them. I take them places, like to the doctor. I get them to participate in conversations or games and things like that. But it seems that I'm always just meeting the needs of the moment. I'm not sure what the long-range goals of the place are and if anyone, including me, is contributing to them in any way."

Response to self. "You get some satisfaction in providing the services you do, but this lack of overall purpose or direction for yourself and the institution is frustrating. I'm not sure what you're doing about all of this, either at the halfway house or in the counseling program."

Self. "I'm letting myself get frustrated, irritated, and depressed. I'm down on myself and down on the people who run the house. It's a day-to-day operation that sometimes seems to be a fly-by-night venture. See! There I go. You're right. I'm not doing anything to handle my frustrations. I am doing something to try to better myself, that is, to make myself a better helper, but this is the first time I've expressed myself about the halfway house or about the counseling program."

Response to self. "You'd have to stop to think what to do."

Self. "Right. I don't want to go off half cocked. But I could share my concerns about the psychology program with one of the instructors. She teaches the second-year trainees. She gave a very practical talk. I could also see whether my concerns are shared by my classmates. I could also talk to the second-year students to get a feeling for how practical next year might be. I feel more at a loss at the halfway house. I don't want to come across as the wet-behind-the-ears critic."

Response to self. "Anyone you trust there?"

Self. "Not that I can think of. . . . But there is a consultant who shows up once in a while. He runs staff meetings in a very practical way. Maybe I can get hold of him and get a wider picture."

Response to self. "So, overall?"

Self. "I've got some work to do before I rush to judgment. I like the fact that I want the people and the institutions in the profession to be competent. Deep down I think that I'd make a good helper. I say to myself, 'You're all right; you're trying to do what is right.' Also, I need to challenge my idealism. I spend too much time grieving over what is happening at school and at the halfway house. I need to figure out how to turn minuses into pluses."

1. Review this trainee's responses to himself in a small group. What kinds of responses did he use? How would you evaluate their quality? Did they get him someplace? Describe the movement he made during the session. What responses would you have changed?
2. Choose a problematic area that is important to you and on separate sheets of paper engage in the same kind of dialogue with yourself. Tell your story briefly, choose a high-leverage issue, and clarify it in terms of specific experiences, behaviors, and feelings. Stay within the steps of Stage I.
3. In groups of three, share your dialogue and give one another feedback on its quality.

SUMMARIZING AND FOCUS

At a number of points throughout the helping process it is useful for helpers to summarize or to have clients summarize the principal points of their interactions. This places clients under pressure to focus and move on. At Step I-C, this means moving on toward the development of new scenarios, setting goals, and problem-managing action. Thus, summarizing can be an effective way of helping a client move from Stage I to Stage II.

EXERCISE 48: SUMMARIZING AS A WAY OF PROVIDING FOCUS

This exercise assumes that trainees have been using the skills and methods of Steps I-A and I-B to help one another.

1. The total training group is divided into subgroups of three.
2. There are three roles in each subgroup: helper, client, and observer.
3. The helper spends about eight to ten minutes counseling the client. The client should continue to explore one of the problem areas he or she has chosen to deal with in the training group.
4. At the end of four minutes, the helper summarizes the principal points of the interaction. Helpers should try to make the summary both accurate and concise. The helper can draw on past interactions if he or she is counseling a "client" whom he or she has counseled before. At the end of eight minutes or so, the helper should engage in a second summary.
5. At the end of each summary, the helper should ask the <u>client</u> to draw some sort of implication or conclusion from the summary. That is, the client is asked to take the next step.
6. Then both observer and client give the helper feedback as to the accuracy and the helpfulness of the summary. The summary is helpful if it moves the client toward problem clarification, goal setting, and action.
7. This process is repeated until each person in the subgroup has had an opportunity to play each role.

Example 1

It would be too cumbersome to print ten minutes of dialogue here, but consider this brief outline of a case.

A young man, 22, has been talking about some developmental issues. One of his concerns is that he sees himself as relating to women poorly. One side of his face is scarred from a fire that occurred two years previous to the counseling session. He has made some previous remarks about the difficulties he has relating to women. After five minutes of interaction, the helper summarizes:

Helper. "Dave, let me see if I have the main points you've been making. First, because of the scars, you think you turn women off before you even get to talk with them. The second point, and I have to make sure that this is what you are saying, is that your initial approach to women is cautious, or cynical, or maybe even subtly hostile since you've come to expect rejection somewhat automatically."

Dave. "Yeah, but now that you've put it all together, I am not so sure that it's all that subtle."

Helper. "You also said that the women you meet are cautious with you. Some might see you as 'mean.' Some steer clear of you because they see you as a kind of 'difficult person.' What closes the circle is that you take their caution or aloofness as their being turned off by your physical appearance."

Dave. "I don't like to hear it that way, but that's what I've been saying."

Helper. "If these points are fairly accurate, I wonder what implication you might see in them."

Dave. "I'm the one that rejects me because of my face. Nothing's going to get better until I do something about that."

Note that the client draws an implication from the summary ("I am the primary one who rejects me") and moves on to some minimal declaration of intent ("I need to change this").

Example 2

A woman, 47, has been talking about her behavior in the training group. She feels that she is quite nonassertive and that this stands in the way of being an effective helper. She and her helper explore this theme for a while and then the helper gives the following summary:

Helper. "I'd like to take a moment to pull together the main points of our conversation. You're convinced that the ability to 'intrude' reasonably into the life of the client is essential for you as a helper. However, this simply has not been part of your normal interpersonal style. If anything, you are too hesitant to make demands on anyone. When you take the role of helper in training sessions, you feel awkward using even basic empathy and even more awkward using probes. As a result, you let your clients ramble and their problems remain unfocused. Outside training sessions you still see yourself as quite passive, except now you're much more aware of it. If this is more or less accurate, what implication might you draw from it?"

Client. "When I hear it all put together like that, my immediate reaction is to say that I shouldn't try to be a counselor. But I think I would be selling myself short. No matter what my career will be, I can't keep on being such a hesitant person. I have to learn how to take risks."

In the client's new scenario, she is a risk taker.

After each trainee gives his or her summary and elicits some reaction from the client, the feedback from the client and the observer should center on the accuracy and the usefulness of the summary, not on a further exploration of the client's problem. Recall that feedback is most effective when it is clear, concise, behavioral, and nonpunitive.

PART FIVE

STAGE II: DEVELOPING PREFERRED SCENARIOS AND SETTING GOALS

Although helping clients tell their stories, challenge blind spots, and choose key issues for management are all important, it is just as important to help them develop preferred scenarios and set goals. Problem clarification and ownership need to be translated into problem-managing and opportunity-developing goals. A preferred scenario is a goal or a package of goals. What would this problem look like if it were being managed better? A goal is what a client wants to accomplish in order to manage a problem situation more effectively. Goals are to be distinguished from the strategies used to achieve goals. New scenarios and goals deal with **what** is to be accomplished, while strategies for action deal with **how** a goal is to be accomplished. For instance, if a person wants to stop drinking, then "a life without alcohol" is his or her new scenario or goal. But there are many paths to the accomplishment of this goal.

STEP II-A: DEVELOPING NEW-SCENARIO POSSIBILITIES

Effective helping is related to the use of imagination. In this step you are asked to help yourself and clients develop a vision of a better future. Once clients understand the nature of the problem situation, they need to ask themselves, "What would my situation look like if it were better, at least a little bit better?"

EXERCISE 49: DEVELOPING NEW SCENARIOS: PICTURES OF A BETTER FUTURE

In this exercise you are asked to use your imagination to build better "futures" for yourself as a way of preparing you to help others develop new scenarios.

Example

Since most students do not operate at 100% efficiency, there is usually room for improvement in the area of learning. Luisa, a junior beginning her third year of college, is dissatisfied with the way she goes about learning. She decides to use her imagination to invent a new study scenario. She brainstorms preferred-scenario possibilities, that is, goals that would constitute her new learning style. Using the future tense, she comes up with the following list:

* I will not be studying for grades, but studying to learn. Paradoxically this might help my grades, but I will not be putting in extra effort just to raise a B to an A.
* I will be a better contributor in class, not in the sense that I will be trying to make a good impression on my teachers. I will do whatever I need to do to learn. This may mean placing more demands on teachers to clarify points, making more contributions, and involving myself in discussions with peers.
* I will have in place a more constructive approach to writing papers. For instance, once a paper is assigned, I will start a file on the topic and collect ideas, quotes, and data as I go along. Then, when it comes to writing the paper, I will not have to try to create something out of nothing at the last moment. I assume this will help me feel better about the paper and about myself.
* I will be reading more broadly in the area of my major, psychology, not just the articles and books assigned but also in the areas of my interest. I will let my desire to know drive my learning.

Luisa goes on to draw up a fairly extensive list of the patterns of behavior that might have a place in her new scenario, that is, her new approach to learning. Only when she has an extensive list does she address the task of evaluating and choosing the actual goals that will constitute her new learning style.

1. Read Chapter Eleven in the text on developing new scenarios.
2. Choose two problem or undeveloped-opportunity areas on which you have been working.
3. Like Luisa, brainstorm possibilities for a better future in these two areas.
4. Use the following questions to help yourself develop preferred-scenario possibilities:

   * What would the current problem look like if it were better?
   * What would I be doing that I'm not doing now?
   * What would I stop doing that I am doing now?
   * What accomplishments would exist that do not exist now?
   * What would be fractionally better? What would be substantially better? What would be dramatically better?
   * What goals would be in place that are not in place now?

Problem area #1. _____

_____

_____

Problem area #2. _____

_____

_____

_____

5. On separate sheets of paper, brainstorm a number of possible goals for each problem area.
6. In a format suggested by your instructor, give feedback to and get feedback from one or two

other members of the training group. The feedback should deal with the number of possibilities and their linkage to the original problem situation.

EXERCISE 50: HELPING OTHERS DEVELOP NEW-SCENARIO POSSIBILITIES

In this exercise, you are asked to help one of the other members of your group develop new-scenario possibilities.

1. Choose a partner for this exercise.
2. One partner takes the role of client and the other the role of the helper.
3. The client gives a summary of one of the problem situations focused on in the previous exercise.
4. The client then shares his or her list of new-scenario possibilities (the ones developed in the previous exercise).
5. The helper, using empathy, probes, and challenges, helps the client clarify and add to the items already on the list. Overall, the helper helps the client tap into his or her imagination more fully.
6. After ten minutes, the helper gets feedback from the client as to how useful he or she has been.
7. Switch roles and repeat the process.

Example

In the following example, Geraldo, a business-major junior in college, has given a summary of the problem situation and his list of preferred-
scenario possibilities. His uncle, who runs a small business, has offered to teach him the ropes. While such an opportunity fits perfectly with his career plans, Geraldo has done nothing to develop it. Other things such as studies, intramural sports, and a rather substantial social life have crowded it out. Given his ambitions, Geraldo's priorities are out of line. Trish, his helper, challenges his list.

Trish. "There seems to be a contradiction. Very few of the possibilities you have outlined for a more 'balanced' lifestyle relate to your uncle's offer. Yet earlier you said you wanted to develop the 'serious side' of things a bit more."
Geraldo. "I don't want work to consume my life. I want a balanced life, not like some of those guys that never come home from work."
Trish. "In what way is your life out of balance right now?"
Geraldo. "Well, there's a bit too much play, I suppose."
Trish. "If that's the case, let's brainstorm more work-related possibilities. You can take care of the balance when you actually set your agenda. Spell out more possibilities that relate to your uncle's offer. You already said he's not going to push you into anything."
Geraldo. "Let's see. I'd be putting in 10 to 15 hours a week at the plant."
Trish. "What would that look like?"
Geraldo. "Well, I don't know what my uncle has in mind."
Trish. "Name some of the things you'd like to get out of that kind of 'internship.'"
Geraldo. "Oh, I hadn't give much thought to that. . . . Well, I'd like to learn something about the finance part of his business--where the money comes from, what kind of debt he carries, cash flow--all those things that are still too theoretical for me in the courses I'm taking."
Trish. "What else?"
Geraldo. "Everyone's talking about business strategy. I wonder whether he has some sort of strategic plan. Maybe I could work with him to develop one or reformulate the one he's got."
Trish. "That sounds more exciting."
Geraldo. "Yeah. It would certainly send me back to the books in a different way. I saw a couple of articles on new approaches to strategic planning in the Harvard Business Review. But now I'd actually read and study them!"

Trish. "So there could be synergy between the internship and your studies."

Geraldo. "Maybe a lot. There's also a lot of push in the 'soft' side of the business. Things like employee participation."

Trish. "What would you be doing in that area?"

Geraldo. "In an organizational behavior class, the prof talked about and a 'human resources audit' and gave us a methodology for doing one. It means taking stock of people like you'd take stock of other resources. Who are the high flyers? Who are the drones? Making the right decisions about people is easier if you take a systematic look at the work force or at least the key players in it. I could see myself doing something like that."

The dialogue goes on in that vein. Geraldo, with the help of Trish, develops not only a lot of preferred-scenario possibilities but also much more enthusiasm about his uncle's project. Geraldo gives Trish high marks for empathy, probing, and challenge.

STEP II-B: AGENDAS: HELPING CLIENTS SET VIABLE GOALS

Once new-scenario possibilities have been brainstormed, a goal or a package of goals needs to be chosen. This package of goals constitutes the client's **agenda**, literally those things that **need to be accomplished** in order manage the original problem situation. For instance, Geraldo, after brainstorming a number of possibilities for structuring his internship in his uncle's company, chooses four of the possibilities and makes these his agenda. He shares them with his uncle and, after some negotiation, comes up with a revised package they can both live with.

EXERCISE 51:   CHOOSING AGENDA ITEMS FROM BRAINSTORMED POSSIBILITIES

In this exercise you are asked to do what Geraldo had to do--choose several preferred-scenario possibilities as the first step in crafting an agenda. Possibilities should be chosen because they will best help you manage some problem situation or develop some opportunity.

1. Read the following case.

Vanessa, 46, has been divorced for about a year. She has done little to restructure her life and is still in the doldrums. At the urging of a friend, she sees a counselor. With her help, she brainstorms a range of preferred-scenario possibilities around the theme of "my new life as a single person." She is currently a salesperson in the women's apparel department of an moderately upscale store. She lives in the house that was part of the divorce settlement. She has no children. When she finally decided that she wanted children, it was too late. There was some discussion about adopting a child, but it didn't get very far. The marriage was disintegrating. Her visits to the counselor have reawakened (or at least awakened) a desire to take charge of her life and not just let it happen. She let her marriage happen, as it were, and it fell apart. She is not filled with anger at her former husband. If anything, she's a bit too down on herself. Her grieving is filled with self-recrimination. Below are some of the possibilities she has brainstormed. These are the goals she would like to accomplish, the patterns of behaviors she would like to see in place, the sets of behaviors she would like to get rid of.

2. Mustering all the empathy within you, try to read the list from her point of view (even though you hardly know her!). The helper asked her, "What would your post-divorce life look like if it were better? What would you want to see in place?"

* A job related to the fashion industry; maybe a career later.
* A small condo that will not need much maintenance on my part instead of the house.

* The elimination of poor-me attitudes.
* The elimination of waiting around for things to happen.
* The development of a social life. For the time being, a range of friends rather than potential husbands. A couple of good women friends.
* Getting into physical shape.
* A hobby or avocation that I could get lost in. Something with substance.
* Some sort of volunteer work. With children, if possible.
* Some religion-related activities, not necessarily established-church related. Something that deals with the "bigger" questions.
* Some real "grieving" work over the divorce instead of all the self-recrimination.
* Resetting my relationship with my mother (who strongly disapproved of the divorce).
* Getting over a deep-seated fear that my life is going to be bland, if not actually bleak.
* Possibly some involvement with politics.

3. Since Vanessa cannot possibly do all of these or even a substantial package of them all at once, she has to make some choices. Put yourself in her place. Which items would you include in your agenda? On separate pages of paper, indicate the items and your reasons for choosing each. In what way would the agenda item, if accomplished, help manage the overall problem situation?

4. In a small group, share your "package" with the other group members. After all the packages have been shared, discuss the differences in and the reasons for the choices. Note that there is no one right package.

EXERCISE 52: TURNING AIMS INTO GOALS

This exercise assumes that you are familiar with the material on aims and goals in Chapter Eleven. Many clients are more likely to pursue goals if they are clear and specific. Your job here is to move from the general to the specific.

Example

Context. Tom, 42, and his wife, Carol, 39, have been talking to a counselor about how poorly they relate to each other. They have agreed to stop blaming each other, have explored their own behavior in concrete ways, have developed a variety of new perspectives on themselves as both individuals and spouses, and now want to do something about what they have learned.

Without having specific information about the issues Tom and Carol have discussed, use your imagination to come up with four levels of concreteness in a goal-shaping process that might apply to their situation. That is, choose four levels of concreteness (from a mere statement of intent to a concrete and specific goal) that you think someone in their position might choose. Obviously, in an actual counseling situation, you would be helping them shape their own goals. This exercise deals with goals (who is to be done), not with action strategies (how any specific goal is to be accomplished). What follows is Tom and Carol's first shot at moving from a vague to a more specific goal.

Level I: Declaration of intent. "We've got to do something about saving our marriage because it is worth saving."

Level II: General aim. "We'd like to improve the quality of the time we spend together at home."

Level III: More specific aim. "We want to have better give-and-take, problem-solving (rather than accusatory) conversations with each other."

Level IV: Specific goal. "Over the next month, we want to cut in half the number of times our conversations turn into arguments or out-and-out fights."

Note that each level becomes more specific in some way. Note, too, that their specific goal is negative; they do not say what they'd like to put in place of fighting. This might be a flaw in the agenda-setting process. Now do the same with the situations listed below.

1. Use your imagination to develop aims and goals. Get inside the client's mind and try to think the way the client might think.
2. Move from a statement of intent to a specific goal in each case.

1. **Context.** Linda W., 68, is dying of cancer. She has been talking to a pastoral counselor about her dying. One of her principal concerns is that her husband does not talk to her about her impending death. She has a variety of feelings about dying that well up from time to time such as disbelief, fear, resentment, anger, and even peace and resignation. She also has thoughts about life and death that she has never had before and has never shared with anyone.

Statement of intent._____

_____

General aim._____

_____

More specific aim._____

_____

Specific goal._____

_____

_____

2. **Context.** Troy, 30, has been discussing the stress he has been experiencing during this transitional year of his life. Part of the stress relates to his job. He has been working as an accountant with a large firm for the past five years. He makes a decent salary, but he is more and more dissatisfied with the kind of work he is doing. He finds accounting predictable and boring. He doesn't feel that there's much chance for advancement in this company. Many of his associates are much more ambitious than he is.

Statement of intent._____

_____

General aim._____

_____

More specific aim. _____

_____

Specific goal. _____

_____

_____

3. **Context.** Joan, 32, is married and has two small children. Her husband has left her and she has no idea where he is. She has no relatives in the city and only a few acquaintances. She is talking to a counselor in a local community center about her plight. Since her husband was the breadwinner, she now has no income and no savings on which to draw.

Statement of intent. _____

_____

General aim. _____

_____

More specific aim. _____

_____

Specific goal. _____

_____

_____

4. **Context.** Nancy, 19, unmarried, is facing the problem of an unwanted pregnancy. She has a variety of problems. Her parents are extremely upset with her. Her father won't even talk to her. She lives at home and is attending a local community college. These living arrangements are now unsatisfactory to her. Since, for value reasons, she has decided against an abortion, she does not want to live out the remaining months of pregnancy in an atmosphere of hostility and conflict. She is upset because her education is going to be interrupted and finishing college has always been high on her list of priorities. She is unsure about her finances and resents being financially dependent on her parents.

Statement of intent. _____

_____

General aim. _____

More specific aim._____

Specific goal._____

5. **Context.** Julian, 51, a man separated from his wife for seven years, has just lost a son, 19, in an automobile accident. He (Julian) was driving with his son when they were struck by a car that veered into them from the other side of the road. Julian, who had his seat belt fastened, escaped with only cuts and bruises. His son was thrown through the windshield and killed instantly. The driver of the other car is still in critical condition and may or may not live. Now, ten days after the accident, Julian is still in psychological shock and plagued with anger, guilt, and grief. He has not gone back to work and has been avoiding relatives and friends because he finds getting sympathy "painful."

Statement of intent._____

General aim._____

More specific aim._____

Specific goal._____

6. **Context.** Felicia, 44, finds that her nonassertiveness is causing her problems. She is especially bothered at work. She finds that a number of people in the office feel quite free to interrupt her when she is in the middle of a project. She gets angry with herself because her tendency is to put aside what she is doing and try to meet the needs of the person who has interrupted her. As a result, she some times misses important deadlines associated with the projects on which she is working. She feels that others see her as a "soft touch."

Statement of intent._____

General aim_____

_____

More specific aim_____

_____

Specific goal_____

_____

_____

EXERCISE 53: HELPING CLIENTS SHAPE THEIR GOALS

Here are some criteria that can be used as "tools" to help clients shape their goals. As noted in the text, not all clients will need the kind of shaping described here, but many will benefit from it.

* It must be stated as an <u>accomplishment</u>, an outcome, an achievement, rather than a program.
* It must be behaviorally <u>clear and specific</u>.
* It must be <u>measurable or verifiable</u>.
* It must be <u>realistic</u>, that is, within the control of the client, within his or her resources, and environmentally possible. To be motivationally realistic, the goal should have some <u>appeal</u>.
* It must be <u>substantive</u>, that is, if accomplished, it should contribute in some substantive way to handling the problem situation or some part of it.
* It must be in keeping with the <u>values</u> of the client.
* It must be set within a <u>reasonable time frame</u>.

1.   Return to the specific goals you have come up with in each of the cases in the previous exercise (#52) and see if each of these criteria is fulfilled for each goal.
2. If the goal does not meet these standards, use these criteria as tools to shape it until it does.

Example

Tom and Carol's specific goal is: "Over the next month, we want to cut in half the number of times our conversations turn into arguments or out-and-out fights."

*   **Accomplishment.**   "Number of fights <u>decreased</u>" is an accomplishment.   A new pattern of behavior would be <u>in place</u>.
*   **Clarity.**   It is behaviorally <u>clear</u>. They can get a picture of themselves not arguing or fighting. It probably would help if they were more specific, that is, if they actually talked about what an aborted fight or argument would look like. Moreover, it is not clear what they will be doing instead of fighting, such as substituting some kind of problem-solving or negotiation dialogue.
*   **Verifiability.** Since they have some idea of how often they fight per day or week, they can verify whether the number of fights has decreased. At this point, just some kind of counting might be in order. The goal says nothing about the intensity or viciousness of fights. Perhaps that should have been taken into account.

* **Realism.** Tom cannot control his wife's behavior but he can control his own. The same can be said of Carol. The assumption is that both of them have the self-management skills and the emotional resources to back off from fights. Nor do they have any experience in cutting off fights before they begin. Furthermore, neither has something that they are going to put in place of fighting. In what ways does "number of fights decreased" appeal to both of them? There are some problems with realism here.
* **Substance.** It makes sense to suppose that a decrease in the number of arguments or fights will contribute substantially to the betterment of their relationship. However, stopping fighting leaves a void. They had better talk about the void.
* **Values.** They both espouse give-and-take and fairness in their relationship, but they have been poor at delivering. They need to discuss common values that can be used as stimuli for action and criteria for making decisions, especially when things get hot.
* **Time frame.** "Over the next month" is the time frame. They have to determine whether this is a realistic time frame or whether they should move more to some kind of phasing out of unwanted behaviors (together with phasing in the behaviors that are to take the place of the unwanted ones).

Restated goal. "We'd like to reduce the number of arguments or fights we have from an average of two per day to two per week. Each time we avoid fighting, we'd like to declare "time out" and see if we can identify what has led up to the possible fight. This will not be a who's-to-blame session. Rather we want to find out what the process is that leads to all the fighting. We would like, then, to move to a problem solving mode, using the helping model to grapple with the 'hot' issues. If and when we do this, we would like to end by asking ourselves, 'What have we learned from out aborted fight.'"

1. In a small-group setting critique the process Tom and Carol went through. How well did they use the tools to reshape their goal? What do you think of the restated goal? How would you restate the goal?
2. Review each of the goals you came up with in the previous exercise, apply the goal-setting criteria and restate each each goal so that it conforms to these criteria.

EXERCISE 54: SHAPING GOALS FOR YOURSELF

In this exercise you are asked to relate the process of Exercise 53 to some of your own concerns or problems.

1. Return to Exercise 49 in which you developed new-scenario possibilities for problem situations you are currently working on.
2. Take these possibilities and see whether they are statements of intent, general aims, more specific aims, or specific goals. If they are not specific goals, shape them so that they are.

Example

Area of concern. Jeff, a trainee in a counseling psychology program, has been concerned that he does not have the kind of assertiveness that he now believes helpers need in order to be effective in consultations with clients. He is specifically concerned about the quality of his participation in the training group. He comes up with the following:

Level I: Declaration of intent. "I need to be more assertive if I expect to be an effective helper."
Level II: General aim. "I want to take more initiative in this training group."
Level III: More specific aim. "In our open-group sessions, when there is relatively little structure, I want to speak up without being asked to do so."

Level IV: Specific goal. "In the next training session, without being asked to do so, I will respond to what others say with empathy. During our two-hour meeting, I will respond at least ten times with basic empathy when other members talk about themselves."

Jeff applies the criteria for effective goals to his Level-IV statement:

* "This goal is an <u>accomplishment</u>, that is, a pattern of assertive responding <u>in place</u>."
* "It is <u>clear</u>. I can actually picture myself using empathy."
* "It is quite easy to <u>verify</u> whether I have accomplished my goal or not. I can get feedback from the other members of the group and from the trainer."
* "I have the skill of empathy but do not use it often enough. I can summon up the guts needed to use the skill. Therefore, the goal is <u>realistic</u>."
* "Responding with empathy with some frequency will help me develop, at least in part, the kind of assertiveness called for in helping. In this sense, my goal is a <u>substantive</u> step forward."
* "This goal is in keeping with my <u>values</u> of being a good listener and of taking responsibility for myself as a trainee. The value of being an assertive, proactive helper, discussed in Chapter Three of THE SKILLED HELPER, is new to me. While I espouse the idea, I need to work at making this value my own. My goal is a step in this direction."
* "I believe that I can put this new pattern in place within three meetings. I see the <u>time frame</u> as reasonable."

3. In the total training group, briefly criticize this specific goal and Jeff's analysis of it.
4. In a small group, share three preferred-scenario possibilities that you have reshaped into viable goals. Get feedback from your co-learners on how well you have accomplished this task.

EXERCISE 55: HELPING OTHERS SET VIABLE GOALS

In this exercise you are asked to act as a helper/consultant to one of the members of your training group.

1. The total group is to be divided up into smaller groups of three.
2. There are three roles: client, helper, and observer. Decide the order in which you will play each role.
3. The client summarizes some problem situation and then declares his or her <u>intent</u> to do something about the problem or some part of it.
4. The helper, using empathy, probing, and challenging, helps the client move from this statement of intent to a specific problem-managing or opportunity-developing goal that has all seven characteristics listed above.
5. When the helper feels that he or she has fulfilled this task, the session is ended and both observer and client give feedback to the helper on his or her effectiveness.
6. Repeat the process until each person has played each role.

EXERCISE 56: RELATING GOALS TO ACTION

The best goals are those that sit, as it were, on the edge of action. One sign of a well-crafted goal is that the ways of accomplishing it begin to suggest themselves without any explicit consideration of action strategies. Good goals breed action strategies.

1. Read the following case. Think of what needs to be in place if the problems outlined here are to be managed.

Lane, the 15-year-old son of Troy and Rhonda Washington, was hospitalized with what was diagnosed as an "acute schizophrenic attack." He had two older brothers, both teenagers, and two younger sisters, one 10 and one 12, all living at home. The Washingtons lived in a large city. Although both worked, their combined income still left them pinching pennies. They also ran into a host of problems associated with their son's hospitalization: the need to arrange ongoing help and care for their son, financial burdens, behavioral problems among the other siblings, stigma in the community ("They're a funny family with a crazy son," "What kind of parents are they?"), and marital conflict. To make things worse, they did not think the psychiatrist and psychologist they met at the hospital took the time to understand their concerns. They felt that the helpers were trying to push their son back out into the community; in their eyes, the hospital was "trying to get rid of him." "They give him some pills and then give him back to you," was their complaint. No one explained to them that short-term hospitalization was meant to guard the civil rights of patients and avoid the negative effects of long-term institutionalization.

When their son was discharged, they were told that he might have a relapse, but they were not told what to do about it. They had the prospect of caring for Lane in a climate of stigma without adequate information, services, or relief. Feeling abandoned, they were very angry with the mental-health establishment. They had no idea what they should do to respond to his illness or to the range of family problems that had been precipitated by the episode. By chance, they met someone who worked for the National Alliance for the Mentally Ill (NAMI), "an advocacy and education organization that now has more than 850 local affiliates throughout the United States and represents more than 70,000 families" (Backer & Richardson, 1989, p. 547). This person referred them to an agency that provided support and help.

2. Next, consider the following set of aims/goals--patterns of behavior or accomplishments that need to be in place if the problem situation is to be managed. After reading each aim/goal statement, do two things: (a) indicate what further shaping it needs in order to become a viable goal, and (b) in the blanks, jot down some <u>actions</u> you think the Washingtons might be able to take to make the goal a reality.

Research shows that families like the Washingtons want some combination of information, education, opportunities for emotional ventilation and support, professional availability during times of crisis, and contact with other families who have similar difficulties. They wish to understand what constitutes reasonable expectations for them to have for their ill relative and how they can be helpful in his or her recovery [Bernheim, p. 562].

Now, looking through the eyes of this family, see what actions you might take to accomplish the following aims/goals.

a. **The home environment.** The Washingtons will have in place an environment in which the needs of all the members the family are balanced. The home will not be an extension of the hospital. Lane will be taken care of but the needs of the other children will not be ignored. Rhonda and Troy will be attending to their own needs also.

Possible actions._____

_____

_____

_____

_____

_____

121

b. **Care outside the home.** A service program for Lane will be in place. That is, possible services will be reviewed, relevant services identified, and access to these services together with payment will be arranged. Also the logistics of getting Lane to and from hospital appointments will be seen to.

Possible actions. _____

_____

_____

_____

_____

c. **Care inside the home.** Family members will have learned how to cope with Lane's residual symptoms. He might be withdrawn or aggressive, but they will know how to relate to him and help him handle behavioral problems. They will know how to care for him without turning the home into a hospital.

Possible actions. _____

_____

_____

_____

_____

d. **Prevention.** Family members will have been taught to spot early warning symptoms of impending relapse. They will have a program to follow when they see such signs. The program will include such things as contacting the clinic or, in the case of more severe problems, arranging for an ambulance or the police.

Possible actions. _____

_____

_____

_____

_____

e. **Family stress.** They will have learned how to cope with the increased stress all of this will entail. They will have forums for working out their problems. Blow-ups with one another will decrease and those that happen will be managed without damage to fabric of the family.

Possible actions._____

_____

_____

_____

_____

_____

f. **Stigma.** Special attention will be paid to managing whatever stigma might be attached to Lane's illness. Families members will know whom to tell, what to say, how to respond to inquiries, and how to deal with blame and insults.

Possible actions._____

_____

_____

_____

_____

_____

g. **Limitation of grief.** The normal guilt, anger, frustration, fear, and grief that goes with problem situations like this will be resolved or managed.

Possible actions._____

_____

_____

_____

_____

_____

STEP II-C: HELPING CLIENTS COMMIT THEMSELVES TO PREFERRED-SCENARIO GOALS

Many of us choose goals that will help us manage problems and develop opportunities, but we do not explore them from the viewpoint of commitment. Just because goals are tied nicely to the original problem situation and initially are espoused by us does not mean that we are really committed to them nor that we will follow through. The work of discusssing problems and setting goals to manage them is costly in terms of time, psychological effort, and expense. A direct consideration of commitment can raise the probability that clients will actually pursue these goals.

EXERCISE 57: REVIEWING THE COST/BENEFIT RATIO IN THE CHOICE OF GOALS

In most choices we make there are both benefits and costs. Commitment to a preferred-scenario goal often depends on a favorable cost/benefit ratio. Do the benefits outweigh the costs?

Example

In January, Helga, a married woman with two children, one a senior in college and one a sophomore, was told that she had an advanced case of cancer. She was also told that a rather rigorous series of chemotherapy treatments might prolong her life, but they would not save her. She desperately wanted to see her daughter graduate from college in June, so she opted for the treatments. Although she found them quite difficult, she bouyed herself up by the desire to be at the graduation. Although in a wheel chair, she was there for the graduation in June. When the doctor suggested that she could now face the inevitable with equanimity, she said: "But, doctor, in only two years my son will be graduating."

This is a striking example of a woman's deciding that the costs, however high, were outweighed by the benefits. Obviously, this is not always the case. This exercise gives you the opportunity to explore your goals from a cost-benefit perspective. Is it worth the effort? What's the payoff?

1. Divide up into pairs, with one partner acting as client, one as helper.
2. Help your partner review one of the goals of his or her agenda from a cost/benefit perspective. The helper is to use basic empathy, probing, and challenging to help his or her partner do this. Help your partner identify benefits and costs and do some kind of trade-off analysis such as the balance-sheet technique (see the text).
3. Help you partner clearly state the incentives and payoffs that enable him or her commit to the specified goals.
4. After the discussion, each is to get a new partner, change roles, and repeat the process.

EXERCISE 58: MANAGING YOUR COMMITMENT TO YOUR GOALS

In this exercise you are asked to review the goals you have chosen to manage some problem situation with a view to examining your commitment. It is not a question of challenging your good will. All of us, at one time or another, make commitments that are not right for us.

1. Review the problem situation you have been examining and the preferred-scenario goals you have established for yourself as a way of managing it or some part of it.
2. Review the material on choice and commitment in the text and then use the following questions to gauge your level of commitment:

* To what degree are you choosing this goal freely?
* Are your goals chosen from among a number of possibilities?
* How highly do you rate the appeal of your goals?
* Name any ways in which your goals do not appeal to you.
* What's pushing you to choose these goals?
* If any of your goals are imposed by others, rather than freely chosen, what incentives are there besides mere compliance?

3. Choose a partner from your training group.

4. With your partner, review your principal learnings from answering the above questions about two of your preferred-scenario goals. Take turns. Use empathy, probes, and challenges to help one another explore levels of commitment.

5. If you have any hesitations about committing yourself to a goal, discuss these hesitations with your partner. Use the following questions in the discussion.

* What is your state of readiness for change in this area at this time?
* What difficulties do you experience in committing yourself to your agenda or any part of it?
* What stands in the way of your commitment?
* What can you do to get rid of the disincentives and overcome the obstacles?
* What can you do to increase your commitment?
* To what degree is it possible that your commitment is not a true commitment?
* In what ways can the agenda be reformulated to make it more appealing?
* In what ways does it make sense to step back from this problem
  or opportunity right now? To what degree is the timing poor?

6. Finally, reformulate you agenda in terms of what you have learned from the dialogue.

The Restated Agenda

_____

_____

_____

_____

_____

_____

_____

_____

_____

_____

_____

PART SIX

STAGE III: DEVELOPING ACTION STRATEGIES AND PLANS

Stage II deals with **what** clients would like to accomplish in order to handle problem situations. Stage III, on the other hand, deals with with **how** to do this. In this stage, counselors help clients brainstorm strategies for problem-managing action, choose the strategies that best fit available resources, and formulate plans to accomplish preferred-scenario goals. All the exercises in this section, then, are directed toward the accomplishment of goals.

STEP III-A: DEVELOPING ACTION STRATEGIES

There is usually more than one way to accomplish a goal. However, clients often focus on a single strategy or just a few. The task of the counselor in Step III-A is to help clients discover a number of different routes to goal accomplishment. Clients tend to choose a better strategy or set of strategies if they choose from among a number of possibilities. Read Chapter Fourteen before doing the exercises in this section.

EXERCISE 59: BRAINSTORMING ACTION STRATEGIES FOR YOUR OWN GOALS

Brainstorming is a technique you can use to help yourself and your clients move beyond overly constricted thinking. Recall the rules of brainstorming:

* Encourage quantity. Deal with the quality of suggestions later.
* Do not criticize any suggestion. Merely record it.
* Combine suggestions to make new ones.
* Encourage wild possibilities, "One way to keep to my diet and lose weight is to have my mouth sewn up."
* When you feel you have said all you can say, put the list aside and come back to it later to try once more.

Example

Ira, a retired lawyer in training to be a counselor, is in a high-risk category for a heart attack: some of his relatives have died relatively early in life from heart attacks; he is overweight; he exercises very little; he is under a great deal of pressure in his job; and he smokes over a pack of cigarettes a day. One of his goals is to stop smoking within a month. With the help of a nurse practitioner friend, he comes up with the following list of strategies.

Brainstorming ways to stop smoking:

* just stop cold turkey.
* shame myself into it, "How can I be a helper if I engage in self-destructive practices such as smoking?"
* cut down, one less per day until zero is reached.
* look at movies of people with lung cancer.
* pray for help from God to quit.
* use those progressive filters on cigarettes.
* switch to a brand that doesn't taste good.
* switch to a brand that is so heavy in tars and nicotine that even I see it as too much.
* smoke constantly until I can't stand it any more.
* let people know that I'm quitting.
* put an ad in the paper in which I commit myself to stopping.
* send a dollar for each cigarette smoked to a cause I don't believe in, for instance, the "other" political party.
* get hypnotized; through a variety of post-hypnotic suggestions have the craving for smoking lessened.
* pair smoking with painful electric shocks.
* take a pledge before my minister to stop smoking.
* join a professional group for those who want to stop smoking.
* visit the hospital and talk to people dying of lung cancer.
* if I buy cigarettes and have one or two, throw the rest away as soon as I come to my senses.
* hire someone to follow me around and make fun of me whenever I have a cigarette.
* have my hands put in casts so I can't hold a cigarette.
* don't allow myself to watch television on the days in which I have even one cigarette.
* reward myself with a week-end fishing trip once I have not smoked for two weeks.
* substitute chewing gum for smoking, starting first with nicotine-flavored gum.
* avoid friends who smoke.
* have a ceremony in which I ritually burn whatever cigarettes I have and commit myself to living without them.
* suck on hard candy made with one of the new non-sugar sweeteners instead of smoking.
* give myself points each time I want to smoke a cigarette and don't; when I have saved up a number of points reward myself with some kind of "luxury."

Note that Ira includes a number of wild possibilities in his brainstorming session.

1. Now do the same for two goals you have set for yourself in order to manage some problem situation or develop some opportunity. Make sure that the goal has been properly shaped according to the principles in Step II-B. Vague goals will yield vague strategies.

Goal 1._____

_____

_____

_____

On a separate page, like Ira, brainstorm ways of achieving this goal. Observe the brainstorming rules. When you think you have run out of possibilities, stop and return to the task later.

Goal 2._____

_____

_____

_____

Brainstorm ways of achieving this goal. Add wilder possibilities at the end.

2. After you have finished your list, take one of the goals and the brainstorming list, sit down with one of your fellow trainees, and see if, through interaction with him or her, you can expand your list. Be careful to follow the rules of brainstorming.
3. Switch roles. Through empathy, probing, and challenge, help your partner expand his or her list.
4. In the total group discuss what you have learned about yourself and the brainstorming process.
5. Keep both strategy lists. You will use them in an exercise in Step III-B.

EXERCISE 60: ACTION STRATEGIES: PUTTING YOURSELF IN THE CLIENT'S SHOES

Here are a number of cases in which the client has set a preferred-scenario goal and needs help in determining how to accomplish it. You are asked to put yourself in the client's shoes and brainstorm action strategies that you yourself might think of using were you that particular client.

Example

Richard, 53, has been a very active person, career-wise, physically, socially, and intellectually. In fact, he has always prided himself on the balance he has been able to maintain in his life. However, an auto accident that was not his fault has left him a paraplegic. With the help of a counselor he has begun to manage the depression that almost inevitably follows such a tragedy. In the process of re-directing his life, he has set some goals. Since his job and his recreational activities involved a great deal of physical activity, a great deal of re-direction is called for.

One of his goals is to write a book called "The Book of Hope" about ordinary people who have creatively re-set their lives after some kind of tragedy. The book has two purposes. Since it would be partly autobiographical, it will be a kind of chronicle of his own re-direction efforts. This will help him commit himself to some of the grueling rehabilitation work that is in store for him. Second, since the book would also be about others struggling with their own tragedies, these people will be models for him. Richard has never published anything, so the "how" is more difficult. For him, writing the book is more important than publishing it. Therefore, the anxiety of finding a publisher is not part of the "how."

Hobart is a graduate student in a clinical psychology training program. He says to himself, "If I were Richard, here are some of the things I might do to get the book written."

*   Get a book on writing and learn the basics.
*   Start writing short bits on my own experience, anything that comes to mind.
*   Read books written by those who conquered some kind of tragedy.
*   Talk to the authors of these books.
*   Find out what the pitfalls of writing are. There is no use setting off on a course of action that will only add to my depression.
*   Get a ghost writer who can translate my ideas into words.

* Write a number of very short, to-the-point pamphlets, then turn them into a book.
* Learn how to use a word-processing program both as part of my physical rehabilitation program and as a way of jotting down and playing with ideas.
* Do rough drafts of topics that interest me and let someone else put them into shape.
* Record discussions about my own experiences with the counselor, the rehabilitation professionals, and friends and then have these transcribed for editing.
* Interview people who have turned tragedies like mine around.
* Interview professionals and the relatives and friends of people involved in personal tragedies. Record their points of view.
* Through discussion with friends get a clear idea of what this book will be about.
* Find some way of making it a bit different from similar books. What could I do that would give such a book a special slant?

Now do the same kind of work for each of the following cases.

1. Tad, 27, is gay. He has learned that he is not only HIV positive but that he has ARC (AIDS Related Complex). He is taking the drug AZT and his symptoms have disappeared. Since his family--parents, two brothers, one married, and three sisters, two married--never approved of his lifestyle, he moved to a different city. But now he wants to return to his home town and struggle with his illness where he grew up. One of his goals is reconciliation with his family. There has been very little communication with them, but he did return briefly for two of the weddings. He wants to start the work on reconciliation while he is still feeling well. He realizes that reconciliation is a two-way street and that he cannot set goals for others.

a. **Goal.** If you were Tad, what would "reconciliation with my family" look like? If accomplished what would this goal look like? What would be in place that is not now in place? How is the goal modified by the fact that reconciliation is a two-way street?

_____

_____

_____

_____

_____

_____

_____

_____

b. **Strategies.** What are some of the things you might do to achieve the kind of reconciliation with your family that you have outlined above? Do the brainstorming on a separate sheet of paper.
c. **Different versions of the goal.** In a small group, first share your version of the goal "reconciliation with my family." Discuss the differt ways in which the members of the group expressed the goal. Note that "reconciliation" does not mean the same thing to everyone.
d. **Brainstorming lists.** Each group member shares his or her list. No one criticizes any of the items on any list. Keep your list for use in an exercise in Step III-B.
e. **Learnings.** After hearing all the goals and the strategy list for each, discuss with your fellow group members what you have learned from this exercise.

2. The Martins live in an inner city neighborhood that has become infested with "crack houses" and drug peddlers. They have one son, 11, and one daughter, 8. Their elderly parents live in the area and do not want to leave. The Martins are a poor family and cannot afford housing in a better neighborhood. They have friends in the area, but they are as distressed as the Martins. More and more they fear for their own safety and the safety and well being of their children. They belong to a local church. The minister there has started a one-man crusade against drugs in the area, but he has been threatened and his car has been vandalized several times. A social worker is discussing their concerns with them. Their goal, stated over and over, is their safety and the well being of their children.

a. **Goal.** If you were the Martins, what would the aim "our safety and the well being of our children" look like? What would be in place that is not in place now given the resources they have? Out of a "package" of goals, what would one realistic goal look like?

_____

_____

_____

_____

_____

_____

_____

b. **Strategies.** What are some of the things the Martins might be able to do to achieve the goal as you have just described it? Do the brainstorming on a separate sheet of paper.
c. **Different versions of the goal.** In a small group, first share your versions of the goal the Martin's aim or goal. Discuss the different ways in which the members of the group expressed the goal. How realistic are these goals?
d. **Brainstorming lists.** Share your brainstormed lists of possible strategies without criticizing anyone's suggestions. Keep your list for use in an exercise in Step III-B.
e. **Learnings.** After hearing the goals and all the lists, discuss what you have learned from this exercise.

EXERCISE 61: HELPING OTHERS BRAINSTORM STRATEGIES FOR ACTION

As a counselor, you can help your fellow trainees stimulate their imaginations to come up with creative ways of achieving their goals. In this exercise, use probes and challenges based on questions such as the following:

* **How:** How can you get where you'd like to go? How many different ways are there to accomplish what you want to   accomplish?
* **Who:** Who can help you achieve your goal? What people can serve as resources for the accomplishment of this goal?
* **What:** What resources both inside yourself and outside can help you accomplish your goals?
* **Where:** What places can help you achieve your goal?
* **When:** What times or what kind of timing can help you achieve your goal? Is one time better than another?

Example

What follows are bits and pieces of a counseling session in which Angie, the counselor, is helping Meredith, the client, develop strategies to accomplish one of the goals of his agenda. Meredith procrastinates a great deal. He feels that he needs to manage this problem in his own life if he is to help clients move from inertia to action. His aim is to reduce the amount of procrastination in his life. In exploring his problem, he realizes that he puts off many of the assignments he receives in class. The result is that he is overloaded at the end of the semester, experiences a great deal of stress, does many of the tasks poorly, and receives lower grades than he is capable of. While his overall goal is to reduce the total amount of procrastination in his life, his immediate goal is to be up-to-date every week in all assignments for the counseling course. The major paper for the course is to be finished one full week before it is due. He chooses this course as his target because he finds it the most interesting and has many incentives for doing the work on time. He presents his list of the strategies he has brainstormed on his own to Angie. After discussing this list, their further conversations sound something like this:

Angie. "You said that you waste a lot of time. Tell me more about that."
Meredith. "Well, I go to the library a lot to study, with the best intentions, but I meet friends, we kid around, and time slips away. I guess the library is not the best place to study."
Angie. "Does that suggest another strategy?"
Meredith. "Yeah, study someplace where none of my friends is around. But then I might not . . ."
Angie (interrupting): "We'll evaluate this later. Right now let's just add it to the list."

*   *   *   *   *

Angie. "I know it's your job to manage your own problems, but I assume that you could get help from others and still stay in charge of yourself. What do you think?"
Meredith. "I've been thinking about that. I have one friend . . . we make a bit of fun of him because he makes sure he gets everything done on time. He's not the smartest one of our group, but he gets good grades because he knows how to study. I'd like to pair up with him in some way, maybe even anticipate deadlines the way he does."

*   *   *   *   *

Angie. "Your strategy list sounds a bit tame. Maybe it sounds wild to you because you're trying to change what you do."
Meredith. "I never thought of that. I guess I could get wilder. Hmmm. I could make a contract with my counseling prof to get the written assignments in early! That would be wild for me."

Note here that Angie uses probes dealing with where, who, and wilder possibilities.

1. Divide up into groups of three: client, helper, and observer.
2. Decide in which order you will play these roles.
3. The client will briefly summarize a concern or problem and the preferred-scenario goal that, if accomplished, will help him or her manage the problem. If the preferred scenario is a package of goals, the client will pick one. Make sure that the client states the goal in such a way that it fulfills the criteria for a viable goal.
4. Give the client five minutes to list as many possible ways of accomplishing the goal as he or she can think of. Have the client write them down.
5. Then help the client expand the list. Use probes and challenges based on the questions listed above.
6. Encourage the client to follow the rules of brainstorming:

    *   Do not allow him or her to criticize the suggestions produced.
    *   Encourage your client to expand on the suggestions produced, to piggyback, to combine.
    *   When your client goes dry, encourage him or her to come up with wilder possibilities.

131

* If the client gets stuck, "prime the pump" with a suggestion of your own, but then encourage the client to go on.
* Reinforce your client ("that's good; keep them coming"), not for "good" suggestions, but for sheer quantity.

7. At the end of the session, stop and receive feedback from your client as to the helpfulness of your probes and challenges. Remember the desired outcome is quantity, not quality, of strategies.
8. Switch roles and repeat the process until each has played all three roles.

STEP III-B: HELPING CLIENTS CHOOSE BEST-FIT STRATEGIES

The principle is simple. Strategies for action chosen from a large pool of strategies tend to be more effective than those chosen from a small pool. However, if brainstorming is successful, clients are sometimes left with more possibilities than they can handle. Therefore, once clients have been helped to brainstorm a range of strategies, they might also need help in choosing the most useful. These exercises are designed to help you learn how to help client choose "best-fit" strategies, that is, strategies that best fit the resources, style, circumstances, and motivation level of clients. We begin with you.

EXERCISE 62: A PRELIMINARY SCAN OF BEST-FIT STRATEGIES FOR YOURSELF

You do not necessarily need sophisticated methodologies to come up with a package of strategies that will help you accomplish a goal. In this exercise you are asked to use your common sense to make a "first cut" on the strategies you brainstormed for yourself in Exercise 59.

1. Review the strategies you brainstormed for each of the goals considered in Exercise 59.
2. Star the strategies that make most sense to you. Just use common-sense judgment. Use the following example as a guideline.

Example

Let's return to the case of Ira in Exercise 59. Remember that he is the counselor trainee who wants to stop smoking. Here are the strategies he brainstormed. The ones he chooses in a preliminary common-sense scan are marked with a bullet (o) instead of an asterisk (*).

o just stop cold turkey.
o shame myself into it, "How can I be a helper if I engage in self-destructive practices such as smoking?"
* cut down, one less per day until zero is reached.
* look at movies of people with lung cancer.
o pray for help from God to quit.
* use those progressive filters on cigarettes.
* switch to a brand that doesn't taste good.
* switch to a brand that is so heavy in tars and nicotine that even I see it as too much.
* smoke constantly until I can't stand it any more.
* let people know that I'm quitting.
* put an ad in the paper in which I commit myself to stopping.
* send a dollar for each cigarette smoked to a cause I don't believe in, for instance, the "other" political party.
* get hypnotized; through a variety of post-hypnotic suggestions have the craving for smoking lessened.
* pair smoking with painful electric shocks.
* take a pledge before my minister to stop smoking.

o join a professional group for those who want to stop smoking.
* visit the hospital and talk to people dying of lung cancer.
* if I buy cigarettes and have one or two, throw the rest away as soon as I come to my senses.
* hire someone to follow me around and make fun of me whenever I have a cigarette.
* have my hands put in casts so I can't hold a cigarette.
* don't allow myself to watch television on the days in which I have even one cigarette.
o reward myself with a week-end fishing trip once I have not smoked for two weeks.
o substitute chewing gum for smoking, starting first with nicotine-flavored gum.
* avoid friends who smoke.
* have a ceremony in which I ritually burn whatever cigarettes I have and commit myself to living without them.
* suck on hard candy made with one of the new non-sugar sweeteners instead of smoking.
o give myself points each time I want to smoke a cigarette and don't; when I have saved up a number of points reward myself with some kind of "luxury."

3. Jot down the reasons for the choices you make. Again use Ira's case as a guideline.

Here is Ira's package of common-sense strategies and the reasons for choosing them:

o just stop cold turkey.
o substitute chewing gum for smoking, starting first with nicotine-flavored gum.

"Cutting down doesn't make sense for me. If I'm going to stop I need a clean break. Cutting down involves a protracted period of time during which too many things can go wrong. The gum is a sop to my humanity. I can get rid of that, too. It's a form of gradualism that does not violate my principles."

o shame myself into it, "How can I be a helper if I engage in self-destructive practices such as smoking?"

"This probably could be stated more elegantly. The point is one of values. If I'm going to be a helper, I'd like to make tough decisions. This is a tough decision that makes sense for my health."

o pray for help from God to quit.

"I'm basically a religious person. This will help me put my decision into a larger context. Something like the AA Creed."

o join a professional group for those who want to stop smoking.

"I'm sure that some professionals have some wisdom I could use. It is also a decisive, clean first step. It's a sign that I'm taking this very seriously."

o reward myself with a week-end fishing trip once I have not smoked for two weeks.
o give myself points each time I want to smoke a cigarette and don't; when I have saved up a number of points reward myself with some kind of "luxury."

"These last two make a statement about incentives and rewards. I think I'll do a lot better if I have some incentives for quitting. The biggest incentive will be improved health and knowing I have the guts to make a hard decision. But these other rewards for good behavior also appeal to me."

4. Pick a partner, share the strategies you have starred and the reasons for choosing them.
5. Give each other feedback on the choices made and the reasoning behind the choices.

In this exercise you are asked to put yourself in clients' shoes as they struggle to choose the strategies that will best enable them to accomplish their goals.

1. Review the case of Richard in Exercise 60.
2. Review the strategies that were brainstormed by Hobart, the clinical psychology trainee, who put himself in Richard's shoes:

* Get a book on writing and learn the basics.
* Start writing short bits on my own experience, anything that comes to mind.
* Read books written by those who conquered some kind of tragedy.
* Talk to the authors of these books.
* Find out what the pitfalls of writing are. There is no use setting off on a course of action that will only add to my depression.
* Get a ghost writer who can translate my ideas into words.
* Write a number of very short, to-the-point pamphlets, then turn them into a book.
* Learn how to use a word-processing program both as part of my physical rehabilitation program and as a way of jotting down and playing with ideas.
* Do rough drafts of topics that interest me and let someone else put them into shape.
* Record discussions about my own experiences with the counselor, the rehabilitation professionals, and friends and then have these transcribed for editing.
* Interview people who have turned tragedies like mine around.
* Interview professionals and the relatives and friends of people involved in personal tragedies. Record their points of view.
* Through discussion with friends get a clear idea of what this book will be about.
* Find some way of making it a bit different from similar books. What could I do that would give such a book a special slant?

3. If you have further strategies, add them to the list now.
4. Using your common sense, circle the strategies you believe belong in the best-fit category.
5. Like Ira in Exercise 62, jot down the reasons for your choices.
6. Share your choices and reasons with another trainee and give each other feedback.

EXERCISE 64: USING CRITERIA TO CHOOSE BEST-FIT STRATEGIES

Just as there are criteria for crafting preferred-scenario goals and agendas (Step II-B) so are there criteria for choosing best-fit strategies. The following questions can be asked especially when the client is having difficulty choosing from among a number of possibilities. These criteria complement rather than take the place of common sense.

* **Clarity.** Is the strategy clear?
* **Relevance.** Is it relevant? Will it get me to my goal?
* **Realism.** Is it realistic? Can I do it?
* **Appeal.** Does it appeal to me?
* **Values.** Is it consistent with my values?
* **Efficacy.** Is it effective enough? Does it have bite?

These questions can be recalled through the acronym CRRAVE, on the assumption that clients "crave" to accomplish their goals.

Example

Ira, the counselor trainee who wanted to quit smoking, considered the following possibility on his list: "Cut down gradually, that is, every other day eliminate one cigarette from the 30 I smoke daily. In two months, I would be free."

C - Clarity: "This strategy is very clear; I can actually see the number diminishing. It gets a 6 or 7 for clarity."
R - Relevance: "It leads inevitably to the elimination of my smoking habit, but only if I stick with it. Rating: 3."
R - Realism: "I could probably bring this off. It would be like a game; that would keep me at it. But maybe too much like a game. Rating: 3."
A - Appeal: "I like the idea of easing into it; but I'm quitting because I now am convinced that smoking is very dangerous. I should stop at once. Rating: 1."
V - Values: "There is something in me that says that I should be able to quit cold turkey. That has more 'moral' appeal to me. Gradually cutting down is for 'weaker' people. Rating: 1."
E - Effectiveness: "The more I draw this action program out, the more likely am I to give it up. There are too many pitfalls spread out over a two-month period. Rating: 1."

In summary, Ira says, "I now see that only strategies related to stopping 'cold turkey' have bite." The CRRAVE criteria helped Ira eliminate all strategies related to a gradual reduction in smoking.

1. Read the following case, put yourself in this woman's shoes, and, like Ira, use the CRRAVE criteria for determining the viability of the strategy she proposes.

Case

A young woman has been having disagreements with a male friend. Since he is not the kind of person she wants to marry, her goal is to establish a relationship with him that is less intimate, for instance, one without sexual relations. She knows that she can be friends with him but is not sure if he can be "just" a friend with her. She would rather not lose him as a friend. She also knows that he sees other women. She uses the CRRAVE criteria to evaluate the following strategy: "I'll call a moratorium on our relationship. I'll tell him that I don't want to see him for four months. After that we will be in a better position to re-establish a different kind of relationship, if that's what both of us want."

2. When you have finished, share your ratings and the reasons behind them with a few of your fellow trainees in a small group. In light of Step III-B, discuss your findings. What differences are there? What do you learn from the differences?

3. Now review the reasoning that the woman herself went through and her decision.

DO NOT READ THE NEXT SECTION BEFORE DOING STEPS 1 AND 2 OF THIS EXERCISE!

C - Clarity: "A moratorium is quite clear; it would mean stopping all communication for four months. It would be as if one of us were in Australia for four months. But no phone calls. Rating: 6."
R - Relevance: "Since my goal is moving into a different kind of relationship with him, stepping back to let old ties and behaviors die a bit is essential. A moratorium is not the same as ending a relationship. It leaves the door open. But it does indicate that cutting the relationship off completely could ultimately be the best course. Rating: 6."
R - Realism: "I can stop seeing him. I think I have the assertiveness to tell him exactly what I want and stick to my decision. Obviously I don't know how realistic he will think it is. He might see it as an easy way for me to brush him off. He might get angry and tell me to forget about it. Rating: 4."

135

A - Appeal: "The moratorium appeals to me. It will be a relief not having to manage my relationship with him for a while. Rating: 7."

V - Values: "There is something unilateral about this decision. On the other hand, I do not want to string him along, keeping his hopes for marriage alive. Rating: 4."

E - Effectiveness: "When--and if, because it depends on him, too--we start seeing each other again, it will be much easier to determine whether any kind of meaningful relationship is possible. A moratorium will help determine things one way or another. Rating: 6."

Based on her analysis, she decides to propose the moratorium to her friend.

4. In your small group, discuss her reasoning. In what ways does it differ from your own? If you were her helper, in what ways would you challenge her reasoning and her decision?

EXERCISE 65: USING CRITERIA TO HELP YOURSELF CHOOSE BEST-FIT STRATEGIES

Now carry out the six-step process described below for the key strategies you have starred for yourself. If for some reason you have difficulty making a rating or have some second thoughts about the rating you do assign, circle the rating and review it later with the other members of your training group. When you finish the exercise, you should have a good idea of which possibilities are the best-fit strategies for you.

1. Take one of the lists of possible action strategies you brainstormed for one of your goals in Exercise 59.
2. Add any further possibilities that have come to mind since doing the list.
3. Choose two strategies that (a) are important to you and (b) merit the kind of scrutiny the CRRAVE criteria provide.
4. Use the CRRAVE questions to check the viability of each of the strategies you have starred. Use the 1-7 rating system.
5. Make a choice based on the rating.
6. Finally, share your line of thinking with the members of your small training group. Get feedback from them. Give feedback to others.

Strategy 1

C - Clarity:_____

_____

R - Relevance:_____

_____

R - Realism:_____

_____

A - Appeal:_____

_____

V - Values:_____

E - Effectiveness:_____

_____

Strategy 2

C - Clarity:_____

_____

R - Relevance:_____

_____

R - Realism:_____

_____

A - Appeal:_____

_____

V - Values:_____

_____

E - Effectiveness:_____

_____

EXERCISE 66: CHOOSING BEST-FIT STRATEGIES: THE BALANCE SHEET METHOD

The balance sheet is another tool you can use to evaluate different program possibilities or courses of action. It is especially useful when the problem situation is serious and you are having difficulty rating different courses of action. Review the balance-sheet format on the following page and pp. 348-353 of **THE SKILLED HELPER**.

Example

Background. Rev. Alex M. has gone through several agonizing months reevaluating his vocation to the ministry. He finally decides that he wants to leave the ministry and get a secular job.

His decision, though painful in coming, leaves him with a great deal of peace. He now wonders just how to go about this. One possibility, now that he has made his decision, is to leave immediately. However, since this is a serious choice, he wants to look at it from all angles. He uses the decision balance sheet to do so.

Alex uses the balance sheet to examine the possibility of leaving his position at his present church immediately. We will not present his entire analysis (indeed, each bit of the balance sheet need not be used). Here are some of his key findings.

* **Benefits for me:** Now that I've made my decision, it will be a relief to get away. I want to get away as quickly as possible.

> * **Acceptability:** I have a right to think of my personal needs. I've spent years putting the needs of others and of the institution ahead of my own. I'm not saying that I regret this. Rather, this is now my "season," at least for a while.
> * **Unacceptability:** Leaving right away seems somewhat impulsive to me, meeting my own needs to be rid of a burden.

* **Costs for me:** I don't have a job and I have practically no savings. I'll be in financial crisis.

> * **Acceptability:** My frustration is so high that I'm willing to take some financial chances. Besides, I'm well educated and the job market is good.
> * **Unacceptability:** I will have to forego some of the little luxuries of life for a while, but that's not really unacceptable.

* **Benefits for significant others:** The associate minister of the parish would finally be out from under the burden of these last months. I have been hard to live with. My parents will actually feel better because they know I've been pretty unhappy.

> * **Acceptability:** My best bet is that the associate minister will be so relieved that he will not mind the extra work. Anyway, he's much better than I at getting people involved in the work of the congregation.

* **Costs to significant social settings:** Many of the best programs are not rooted in the church system but in me. If I leave immediately, many of these programs will falter and perhaps die because I have failed to develop leaders from among the members of the congregation. There will be no transition period. The congregation can't count on the associate minister taking over, since he and I have not worked that closely on any of the programs in question.

> * **Acceptability:** The members of the congregation need to become more self-sufficient. They should work for what they get instead of counting so heavily on their ministers.
> * **Unacceptability:** Since I have not worked at developing lay leaders, I feel some responsibility for doing something to see to it that the programs do not die. Some of my deeper feelings say that it isn't fair to pick up and run.

This is enough to give you the flavor of how the balance sheet can be used to explore the acceptability of key goals, subgoals, and, in this case, strategies.

1. Choose a goal for which you have brainstormed strategies.
2. Choose a major strategy or course of action you would like to explore much more fully.
3. Identify the "significant others" and the "significant social settings" that would be affected by your choice.
4. Explore the possible course of action by using the full balance sheet.

If this exercise is to be meaningful, the problem area, the goal, and the strategy or course of action in question must have a good deal of substance to them. Using the balance sheet to make a relatively inconsequential choice is a waste of time.

If I choose this course of action:

The self		
Gains for self:	Acceptable to me because:	Not acceptable to me because:
Losses for self:	Acceptable to me because:	Not acceptable to me because:

Significant others		
Gains for significant others:	Acceptable to me because:	Not acceptable to me because:
Losses for significant others:	Acceptable to me because:	Not acceptable to me because:

Social setting		
Gains for social setting:	Acceptable to me because:	Not acceptable to me because:
Losses for social setting:	Acceptable to me because:	Not acceptable to me because:

Figure 3. The Decision Balance Sheet

STEP III-C: FORMULATING PLANS

An action plan is a step-by-step procedure for accomplishing each goal of an agenda. The strategies chosen in Step III-B often need to be translated into a step-by-step plan. Clients are more likely to act if they know what they are going to do first, what second, what third, and so forth. Realistic time frames for each of the steps are also essential. The plan imposes the discipline clients need to get things done. To prepare for these exercises, read Chapter Sixteen.

EXERCISE 67: FORMULATING A SIMPLE PLAN

Here are the strategies Ira chooses for a stop-smoking program and his reasons for choosing them:

o   just stop cold turkey.
o   substitute chewing gum for smoking, starting first with nicotine-flavored gum.

"Cutting down doesn't make sense for me. If I'm going to stop I need a clean break. Cutting down involves a protracted period of time during which too many things can go wrong. The gum is a sop to my humanity. I can get rid of that, too. It's a form of gradualism that does not violate my principles."

o   shame myself into it, "How can I be a helper if I engage in self-destructive practices such as smoking?"

"This probably could be stated more elegantly. The point is one of values. If I'm going to be a helper, I'd like to make tough decisions. This is a tough decision that makes sense for my health."

o   pray for help from God to quit.

"I'm basically a religious person. This will help me put my decision into a larger context. Something like the AA Creed."

o   join a professional group for those who want to stop smoking.

"I'm sure that some professionals have some wisdom I could use. It is also a decisive, clean first step. It's a sign that I'm taking this very seriously."

o   reward myself with a week-end fishing trip once I have not smoked for two weeks.
o   give myself points each time I want to smoke a cigarette and don't; when I have saved up a number of points reward myself with some kind of "luxury."

"These last two make a statement about incentives and rewards. I think I'll do a lot better if I have some incentives for quitting. The biggest incentive will be improved health and knowing I have the guts to make a hard decision. But these other rewards for good behavior also appeal to me."

1. Pretend that you are Ira. Take these strategies and turn them into a simple step-by-step plan for stopping smoking. What's first? What's second? And so forth. Your statement should begin with the words:

Here's what I'm going to do:

_____

_____

_____

_____

_____

_____

_____

_____

_____

_____

_____

2. Share you plan with one of your fellow trainees.
3. Pool the best features of both plans. Write out the steps of the new one.
4. Hook up with another twosome and share your pooled plan with theirs.
5. Once more incorporate the best features of both in a final plan.
6. Get together with another foursome and compare notes.

EXERCISE 68: SETTING UP THE MAJOR STEPS OF AN ACTION PLAN

Let us return to the case of Richard, the man who wanted to write a book about hope as part of his overall rehabilitation plan after an accident. As you recall, Hobart, putting himself in Richard's shoes, brainstormed the following strategies.

* Get a book on writing and learn the basics.
* Start writing short bits on my own experience, anything that comes to mind.
* Read books written by those who conquered some kind of tragedy.
* Talk to the authors of these books.
* Find out what the pitfalls of writing are. There is no use setting off on a course of action that will only add to my depression.
* Get a ghost writer who can translate my ideas into words.
* Write a number of very short, to-the-point pamphlets, then turn them into a book.
* Learn how to use a word-processing program both as part of my physical rehabilitation program and as a way of jotting down and playing with ideas.
* Do rough drafts of topics that interest me and let someone else put them into shape.
* Record discussions about my own experiences with the counselor, the rehabilitation professionals, and friends and then have these transcribed for editing.
* Interview people who have turned tragedies like mine around.
* Interview professionals and the relatives and friends of people involved in personal tragedies. Record their points of view.
* Through discussion with friends get a clear idea of what this book will be about.
* Find some way of making it a bit different from similar books. What could I do that would give such a book a special slant?

141

1. Place yourself in Richard's shoes.
2. Add further strategies as you see fit.
3. Identify key best-fit strategies.
4. Turn these into the major steps of an overall plan. Focus on the big, rather than the small, step.

_____

_____

_____

_____

_____

_____

_____

_____

_____

_____

5. Share the major steps you have identified with a fellow trainee.
6. Pool your approaches, incorporating them into a revised list of major steps.

EXERCISE 69: SETTING UP THE MAJOR STEPS OF YOUR OWN ACTION PLAN

In this exercise you are asked to establish a plan to accomplish one of the goals you have set for yourself.

Example

Eliza, 38, a widow with two children in their upper teens, wants to get a job. In accomplishment terms, "job obtained and started" is her goal. However, in talking to a counselor, she soon realizes that there are a number of steps in a program leading to the accomplishment of this goal. In putting a plan together, she comes up with the following major steps or subgoals and translates them into "accomplishment" language, that is, what needs to be in place by the end of each step.

* **Step 1: Job criteria established.** She soon discovers that she doesn't want just any kind of job. She has certain standards she would like to meet insofar as this is possible in the current job market.
* **Step 2: Resume developed.** In order to advertise herself well, she needs a high-quality resume.
* **Step 3: Job possibilities canvassed.** She needs to find out just what kinds of jobs are available that meet her general standards.
* **Step 4: A "best-possibilities" list drawn up.** She needs to draw up a list of possibilities that seem most promising in view of the job market and the standards she has worked out.
* **Step 5: Job interviews applied for and engaged in.** This includes sending out her resume. She has to find out whether she wants a particular job and whether the employer wants her.

142

* **Step 6: Best offer chosen and job started.** If she receives two or more offers that meet her standards, she must decide which offer to accept.
* **Contingency plan.** If the kind of job search she designs proves fruitless, she needs to know what she is to do next. She needs a backup plan.

Follow this same process in arranging a multi-step program to achieve one of your own goals.

1. State a goal you would like to accomplish in order to handle some concern or problem situation. For instance, choose one of the goals used in Exercise 62.
2. Review the set of best-fit strategies you have discovered in that exercise.
3. As in the example above, outline the major steps that you must take to accomplish your preferred-scenario goal.
4. Review your plan in a small group to determine how realistic and how potentially effective your plan is.
5. Revise your plan in the light of the feedback you receive.

a. **Goal to be accomplished.** _____

_____

_____

_____

_____

b. **Best-fit strategies for accomplishing the goal.** _____

_____

_____

_____

_____

_____

_____

_____

_____

The major steps of your plan. _____

_____

_____

_____

_____

_____

_____

_____

_____

_____

EXERCISE 70: SUBGOALS: DIVIDE AND CONQUER

If a preferred scenario is complex, for instance, changing careers or doing something about a deteriorating marriage, the plan to achieve it will have a number of major steps or subgoals. In this case a divide-and-conquer strategy is useful. That is, the complex goal (the improvement of the marriage) is divided up into a number of subgoals. These subgoals are the major steps leading to the accomplishment of the overall goal. In a marriage, a more equitable division of household chores might be such a subgoal. It is one goal in the total "package" of goals that will constitute the improved marriage.

Just as with principal goals, a step-by-step process or plan is needed to accomplish each major step or subgoal. For instance, getting a new job, as we have seen, has a number of major steps or subgoals. Each of these major steps, such as getting a resume into shape, calls for its own plan. In this exercise you are asked to pretend that you are Eliza, the widow in Exercise 69 who is looking for a job.

1.   Draw up a plan to accomplish the following major steps of a job-search plan: developing a resume and canvassing job possibilities.

a. **What is the step-by-step process you would engage in to develop a resume?**

_____

_____

_____

_____

_____

_____

_____

b. **What step-by-step process would you use to find out what kind of suitable jobs are available?**

_____

_____

_____

_____

_____

_____

_____

2. Share your plan for each of these in a small group of fellow trainees. As you pool your plans, what steps did you leave out that you think you should have included? What steps did you include that might have been left out?

EXERCISE 71: FORMULATING PLANS FOR THE MAJOR STEPS OF A COMPLEX GOAL

In this exercise you are asked to spell out the action steps for two of the major steps (subgoals) leading up to the accomplishment of some complex goal of your own.

Example

Lynette, a clinical psychology student in a helping-skills training program, has discovered that she comes across as quite manipulative both to her instructors and to her classmates. She believes that she has developed the style as a response to the less than enthusiastic reception she received whenever she encroached on "male" territory, whether at home, school, or in the workplace. However, she realizes that this style is contrary to the values she wants to permeate helper-client relations. She would end up doing to clients what she resents others doing to her. One of the goals she sets in order to manage her manipulative ways is to establish a collaborative style in dealing with teachers, classmates, and clients. This would be a major step in changing her overall manipulative style. The essence of collaboration, as she sees it, is mutual understanding of the issues and mutual decision making. Her current style in working with others is to make the decisions herself while letting the other party <u>think</u> that he or she is having a say.

Here are the steps in her plan to implement this style change:

* Get a very clear picture of the difference between my current style and my preferred style.
* Learn a decision-making process based on mutuality (such as the negotiation process offered by Fisher and Ury in their book <u>Getting to Yes</u>).
* Get a feel for the new style in specific interactions, that is, set up situations in which I can try new behavior.
* Develop a census of the decision-making situations I usually find myself in.
* Prepare myself for each key decision-making interaction.
* Practice mutual decision making in each key decision-making interaction.
* Review with myself how well I actually used the new style.
* Get feedback from the other party from time to time to see whether the process is experienced by others as mutual.

1. Evaluate the steps she has laid out. If she asked you to help her, what feedback would you give her about her plan? What changes would you make?
2. Now do the same for two of the major steps of a plan you have developed to achieve some complex goal related to becoming a more effective helper.

a. A principal goal of mine.

b. One major step in the plan to accomplish this goal.

c. A brief description of the steps I would take to achieve this subgoal.

d. The same goal restated.

e. A second major step in the plan to accomplish this goal.

f. **A brief description of the steps I would take to achieve this subgoal.**

_____

_____

_____

_____

_____

_____

_____

_____

_____

EXERCISE 72: DEVELOPING THE RESOURCES TO IMPLEMENT YOUR PLANS

Plans can be venturesome, but they must also be realistic. Most plans call for resources of one kind or another. In this exercise you are asked to review some of the goals you have established for yourself in previous exercises and the plans you have been formulating to implement these goals with a view to asking yourself, "What kind of resources do I need to develop to implement these plans?" For instance, you may lack the kinds of skills needed to implement a program. If this is a case, the required skills constitute the resources you need.

1. **Indicate a goal** you would like to implement in order to manage some concern or problem situation in some way. Consider the following example. Mark is trying to manage his physical well-being better. He has headaches that disrupt his life. "Frequency of headaches reduced" is one of his goals, a major step toward getting into better physical shape. "The severity of headaches reduced" is another.

2. **Outline a plan** to achieve this goal. Note the parts of the plan that call for resources you may not have or may not have as fully as you would like. Consider Mark once more. Relaxing both physically and psychologically at times of stress and especially when he feels the "aura" that indicates a headache is on its way is one strategy for achieving
his goal.

3. **Indicate the resources** you need to develop to implement the plan. For instance, Mark needs the skills associated with relaxing. He could also benefit from learning how to increase alpha waves, the brain waves associated with relaxation, at times of stress. He does not possess either set of skills. Furthermore, since he allows himself to become the victim of stressful thoughts, he also needs some kind of thought-control skills.

4. **Summarize a plan** that would enable you to develop some of these resources. Mark enrolls in two programs. In one he learns the skills of systematic relaxation and skills related to controlling self-defeating thoughts. In the other, a biofeedback program, he learns how to increase and maintain a high level of alpha waves, especially at times of stress. Fortified with these skills, he is now ready to apply them to a headache-reduction program.

Problem situation #1

a. Your goal or subgoal_____

_____

_____

b. Indicate the part of the plan that calls for skills or other resources that you need to develop or get.

_____

_____

_____

c. Indicate specifically the skills or other resources you need to implement the steps of your plan.

_____

_____

_____

_____

_____

d. Summarize a program or plan that can help you develop or get the resources you need.

_____

_____

_____

_____

_____

Problem situation #2

a. Your goal or subgoal_____

_____

_____

b. Indicate the part of the plan that calls for skills or other resources that you need to develop or get.

_____

_____

_____

_____

c. Indicate specifically the skills or other resources you need to implement the steps of your plan.

_____

_____

_____

_____

_____

d. Summarize a program or plan that can help you develop or get the resources you need.

_____

_____

_____

_____

_____

EXERCISE 73: HELPING OTHERS DEVELOP THE RESOURCES NEEDED FOR PLANS

In this exercise you are asked help clients develop the kinds of resources they need to pursue their principal goals.

1. Mildred and Tom are having trouble with their marriage. They do not handle decisions about finances and about sexual behavior well. Fights dealing with these two areas are frequent. They both agree that their marriage would be better without these fights and they realize that collaborative decision making with respect to sex and finances would be an ideal.

a. What kind of resources do they need to become more collaborative in their decision making?

_____

_____

b. Summarize a program that will help them develop these resources.

_____

_____

_____

_____

_____

c. What resources do they need to make better decisions about money?

_____

_____

d. Summarize a plan that will help them develop these resources.

_____

_____

_____

_____

_____

2. Todd feels bad about his impoverished social life. He is now in his upper twenties and has no intimate female friend and no close friends of either sex. He feels lonely a great deal of the time. Some of the goals he sets for himself involve joining social groups, developing wider circles of acquaintances, and establishing some close friendships.

a. What kind of resources does he need for effective group participation?

_____

_____

b. Summarize a plan that will help him develop these resources.

_____

_____

_____

_____

_____

c. What resources does he need to establish and maintain closer and even intimate relationships?

_____

_____

d. Summarize a plan that might help him develop these resources.

_____

_____

_____

_____

_____

   It goes without saying that, as a counselor, you would not be coming up with plans for clients but rather you would help clients formulate their own plans for developing needed resources.

PART SEVEN

ACTION REVISITED: HELPING CLIENTS PUT STRATEGIES TO WORK

There is a huge difference between talking about action and action itself. Some clients develop challenging goals, excellent strategies, and elegant plans and then stop short of using them effectively to get to their final destinations--valued outcomes, that is, outcomes that make a difference in their lives. Once a workable plan has been developed to accomplish a goal or a subgoal, clients must act, they must implement the plan.

Clients as Tacticians

There are a number of things you can do to help clients act. You can help them become effective tacticians in their everyday lives. In the exercises in this section, tactics, that is, the art or skill of employing available means to accomplish a goal in the face of changing circumstances, is the focus. Tactics is a military term. Not a bad choice, perhaps, because the work of implementing strategies and plans often enough resembles combat. Clients are more likely to implement plans if they can adapt them to changing conditions.

Sustained Action

When clients are trying to manage more complex problem situations, such as a deteriorating marriage or change in lifestyle, then the issue of sustained action is important. They must not only begin to act but continue to act even in the face of temptations to slack off. Clients must live their own lives. You cannot be there to prop them up, nor can the helping relationship go on indefinitely. The exercises in Part Seven will help you prepare clients to grapple with temptations to quit and to sustain problem-managing and opportunity-developing action on their own.

EXERCISE 74: LEARNING FROM FAILURES

As suggested in the text, inertia and entropy dog all of us in our attempts to manage problem situations and develop unexploited opportunities. There is probably no human being who has not failed to carry through on some self-change project. This exercise assumes two things, that we have failed in some self-change project and that we can learn from our failures.

Example

Miguel kept saying that he wanted to leave his father's business and strike out on his own, especially since he and his father had heated arguments over how the business should be run. He earned an MBA in night school and talked about becoming a consultant to small family-run businesses. A medium-sized consulting firm offered him a job. He accepted on the condition that he could finish up some work in the family business. But he always found "one more" project in the family business that needed his attention. All of this came out as part of his "story," even though his main concern was the fact that his woman friend of five years had given him an ultimatum: marriage or forget about the relationship.

Finally, with the help of a counselor, Miguel makes two decisions: to take the job with the consulting firm and to agree to break off the relationship with his woman friend because he is still not seriously entertaining marriage as an immediate possibility.

However, in the ensuing year Miguel never got around to taking the new job. He kept finding tasks to do in his father's company and kept up his running battle with his father. Obviously both of them, in some twisted way, were getting something out of this. As to his relationship with his woman friend, the two of them broke it off four different times during that year until she finally left him and got involved with another man.

Some of Miguel's learnings

Since Miguel and his counselor were not getting anywhere, they decided to break off their relationship for a while. However, when his woman friend definitively broke off their relationship, Miguel was in such pain that he asked to see the counselor again. The first thing the counselor did was to ask Miguel what he had learned from all that had happened, on the assumption that these learnings could form the basis of further efforts. Here are some of his learnings:

* I hate making decisions that have serious action implications.
* I pass myself off as an adventuresome, action-oriented person, but at root I prefer the status quo.
* I am very ambiguous about facing the developmental tasks of an adult my age. I have liked living the life of a 17-year-old at age 30.
* I enjoyed the stimulation of the counseling sessions. I enjoyed reviewing my life with another person and developing insights, but this process involved no real commitment to action on my part.
* Not taking charge of my life and acting on goals has led to the pain I am now experiencing. In putting off the little painful actions that would have served the process of gradual growth, I have ended up in great pain. And it could all happen again.

Notice that Miguel's learnings are about himself, his problem situations, and his way of participating in the helping process.

1. Recall some significant self-change project over the last few years that you abandoned in one way or another.
2. Picture as clearly as possible the forces at work that led to the project's ending in failure, if not with a bang, then with a whimper.
3. In reviewing your failed efforts, jot down what you learned about yourself and the process of change.
4. In groups of four, share your learnings. What themes emerge as the members of the group share their findings?
5. Divide up into dyads. Help each other: (a) discover further lessons in the review of the failed project, and (b) discover what could have been done to keep the project going.

a. **The self-change project that failed.**_____

_____

153

b. Principal reasons for failure.

_____

_____

_____

_____

_____

_____

_____

c. What you learned about yourself and change.

_____

_____

_____

_____

_____

_____

_____

d. What could have been done to keep the project going?

_____

_____

_____

_____

_____

_____

_____

_____

EXERCISE 75: IDENTIFYING AND COPING WITH OBSTACLES TO ACTION

As we have suggested in an earlier exercise, "forewarned is forearmed" in the implementation of any plan. One way of identifying potential pitfalls is the force-field analysis method seen in previous exercises. Another way is to tell yourself the "story" of what you will encounter as you implement a program.

1. Picture yourself trying to implement some action strategy or plan in order to accomplish a problem-managing goal. As in the example below, jot down what you actually see happening.
2. As you tell the story, describe the pitfalls or snags you see yourself encountering along the way. Some pitfalls involve inertia, that is, not starting some step of your plan; others involve entropy, that is, allowing the plan to fall apart over time.
3. Design some kind of plan to handle any significant snag or pitfall you identify.

Example

Justin has a supervisor at work who, he feels, does not like him. He says that she gives him the worst jobs, asks him to put in overtime when he would rather go home, and talks to him in demeaning ways. In the problem exploration phase of counseling, he discovered that he probably reinforces this tendency in her by buckling under, by giving signs that he feels hurt but helpless, and by failing to challenge her in any direct way. He feels so miserable at work that he wants to do something about it. One option is to move to a different department, but to do so he must have the recommendation of his immediate supervisor. Another possibility is to quit and get a job elsewhere, but he likes the company and that would be a drastic option. A third possibility is to deal with his supervisor more directly. He sets goals related to this third option.
One major step in working out this overall problem situation is to seek out an interview with his supervisor and tell her, in a strong but nonpunitive way, his side of the story and how he feels about it. Whatever the outcome, his version of the story would be on record. The counselor asks him to imagine himself doing all of this. What snags does he run into? Some of the things he says are:

* "I see myself about to ask her for an appointment. I see myself hesitating to do so because she might answer me in a sarcastic way. Also, others are usually around and she might embarrass me and they will want to know what's going on, why I want to see her, and all that. I tell myself that I had better wait for a better time to ask."

* "I see myself sitting in her office. Instead of being firm and straightforward, I'm tongue-tied and apologetic. I forget some of the key points I want to make. I let her brush off some of my complaints and in general let her control the interaction."

How can he prepare himself to handle the obstacles or snags he sees in his first statement? Then what could he do in the situation itself?

_____

_____

_____

_____

_____

How can he _prepare_ himself to handle the pitfalls mentioned in his second statement? What could he do _in the situation itself_?

_____

_____

_____

_____

_____

Situation #1

Consider some plan or part of a plan you want to implement. In your mind's eye see yourself moving through the steps of the plan. What obstacles or snags do you encounter? Jot them down.

Obstacles._____

_____

_____

_____

_____

Indicate how you might _prepare_ yourself to handle a significant obstacle or pitfall and what you might do _in the situation itself_ to handle it.

_____

_____

_____

_____

_____

_____

Situation #2

Consider another plan or part of a plan you want to implement. In your mind's eye see yourself moving through the steps of the plan. What obstacles or snags do you encounter? Jot them down.

Obstacles._____

_____

_____

_____

_____

Indicate how you might <u>prepare</u> yourself to handle a significant obstacle and what you might do <u>in the situation itself</u> to handle it.

_____

_____

_____

_____

_____

_____

_____

EXERCISE 76: FORCE-FIELD ANALYSIS AT THE SERVICE OF ACTION

In this exercise you are asked to identify forces "in the field," that is, out there in the clients' day-to-day lives, that might help them implement strategies and plans, together with forces that might hinder them. The former are called "facilitating forces" and the latter "restraining forces." The use of force-field analysis to prepare for action is an application of the adage "forewarned is forearmed."

1. Review a goal or subgoal and the plan you have formulated to accomplish it.
2. Picture yourself "in the field" actually trying to implement the steps of the plan.
3. Identify the principal forces that are helping you reach your goal or subgoal.
4. Identify the principal forces that are hindering you from reaching your goal or subgoal.
5. Share your findings with a partner. Use empathy, probing, and challenge to help each other clarify these two sets of forces.

Example

Ira, as we have seen, wants to stop smoking. He has formulated a step-by-step plan for doing so. Before taking the first step, he uses force-field analysis to identify facilitating and restraining forces in his everyday life.

Some of the facilitating forces identified by Ira:

* my own pride
* the satisfaction of knowing I'm keeping a promise I've made to myself

* the excitement of a new program, the very "newness" of it
* the support and encouragement of my wife and my children
* the support of two close friends who are also quitting
* the good feeling of having that "gunk" out of my system
* the money saved and put aside for more reasonable pleasures
* the ability to jog without feeling I'm going to die

Some of the restraining forces identified by Ira:

* the craving to smoke that I take with me everywhere
* seeing other people smoke
* danger times: when I get nervous, after meals, when I feel depressed and discouraged, when I sit and read the paper, when I have a cup of coffee, at night watching television
* being offered cigarettes by friends
* when the novelty of the program wears off (and that could be fairly soon)
* increased appetite for food and the possibility of putting on weight
* my tendency to rationalize
* the fact that I've tried to stop smoking several times before and have never succeeded

Now do the same for two goals or subgoals you would like to accomplish.

Situation #1

a. Spell out a goal or subgoal you want to accomplish.

_____

_____

_____

b. Picture yourself in the process of implementing the plan formulated to achieve the goal. List the facilitating forces you see "out there" that are helping or could help you to carry out the plan.

_____

_____

_____

_____

_____

_____

_____

_____

_____

c. List the restraining forces that might keep you from carrying out the plan.

_____

_____

_____

_____

_____

_____

_____

_____

Situation #2

a. Indicate a goal or subgoal you want to accomplish.

_____

_____

_____

b. Picture yourself in the process of implementing a plan to accomplish your goal. List the facilitating forces that could help you to implement the plan.

_____

_____

_____

_____

_____

_____

_____

_____

c. List the restraining forces that might hinder you from implementing the plan.

_____

_____

_____

_____

_____

_____

_____

_____

EXERCISE 77: BOLSTERING FACILITATING FORCES

Once you have identified the principal facilitating and restraining forces, you can determine how to bolster critical facilitating forces and neutralize critical restraining forces. In this exercise you are asked to devise ways of bolstering critical facilitating forces.

1. Identify facilitating forces that (a) you see as capable of making a difference in the implementation of a program and (b) you believe you have the resources to strengthen.
2. Formulate a plan for strengthening one or more critical facilitating force. Choose facilitating forces that have a high probability of making a difference in the field.
3. Share your plan with another trainee. Using empathy, probes, and challenges, help each other strengthen the plan.

Example

Klaus is an alcoholic who wants to stop drinking. He joins Alcoholics Anonymous. During a meeting he is given the names and telephone numbers of two people whom he is told he may call at any time of the day or night if he feels he needs help. He sees this as a critical facilitating force--just knowing that help is around the corner when he needs it.
He wants to strengthen this facilitating force.

* First of all, he sees being able to get help anytime as a kind of dependency and so he talks out the negative feelings he has about being dependent in this way with a counselor. In talking, he soon realizes that it is a temporary form of dependency that is instrumental in achieving an important goal, developing a pattern of sobriety.
* Second, he calls the telephone numbers a couple of times when he is not in trouble just to get the feel of doing so.
* Third, he puts the numbers in his wallet, he memorizes them, and he puts them on a piece a paper and carries them in a medical bracelet that tells people who might find him drunk that he is an alcoholic trying to overcome his problem.
* Finally, he calls the telephone numbers a couple of times when the craving for alcohol is high and his spirits are low. That is, he gets used to this as a temporary resource.

160

Situation #1

a. Briefly describe one or two key facilitating forces from Situation #1 in Exercise 76 that you would like to strengthen.

_____

_____

_____

_____

_____

b. Indicate how you would like to go about strengthening these key facilitating forces. What do you plan to do?

_____

_____

_____

_____

_____

_____

_____

_____

_____

_____

_____

Situation #2

a. Briefly indicate one or two key facilitating forces from Situation #2 in Exercise 76 that you would like to strengthen.

_____

_____

_____

_____

_____

b. Briefly indicate how you would like to go about strengthening these key facilitating forces.

_____

_____

_____

_____

_____

_____

_____

_____

EXERCISE 78: DEALING WITH RESTRAINING FORCES

Sometimes, although not always, it is helpful to try to neutralize or reduce the strength of critical restraining forces.

1. Identify critical restraining forces from your list in Exercise 60, that is, restraining forces that (a) if neutralized or reduced, would make a significant difference in the implementation of your plan and (b) you feel you have the ability to neutralize or reduce.
2. Formulate a plan for neutralizing or reducing these restraining forces.
3. Share your plan with another group member and get feedback. Through discussion with him or her, try to improve your plan.

Example

Ingrid is on welfare, but she has a goal of getting a job. Part of her plan is to apply for and go to job interviews. However, she ends up missing a number of the interviews. By examining her behavior, she learns that there are at least two critical restraining forces. One is that she has a poor self-image; she thinks she looks ugly and that the interviewer won't give her a fair chance simply because of her looks. Another is that at the last moment she thinks of a number of "important" tasks that must be done, for instance, visiting her ailing mother, before she can do anything else. She does these tasks instead of going to the interview.

How might Ingrid handle the problem of feeling ashamed of her looks?

_____

_____

_____

_____

_____

How might Ingrid handle the problem of putting "important" tasks ahead of going to job interviews?

_____

_____

_____

_____

_____

Situation #1

a. Briefly indicate one or two critical restraining forces that you identified in Exercise 62 and that you see as critical.

_____

_____

_____

_____

b. What might you do to neutralize or reduce these restraining forces?

_____

_____

_____

_____

Situation #2

a. Briefly indicate one or two key restraining forces that you identified in Exercise 60 and which you see as critical.

_____

_____

_____

_____

b. What might you be able to do to neutralize or reduce these restraining forces?

_____

_____

EXERCISE 79: USING SUPPORTIVE AND CHALLENGING RELATIONSHIPS

Key people in the day-to-day lives of clients can play an important part in helping them stay on track as they move toward their goals. If part of a client's problem is that he or she is "out of community," then a parallel part of the helping process should be to help the client develop human resources in his or her everyday life.

In this exercise you are asked to look at strategies and plans from the viewpoint of these human resources. People can provide both support and challenge.

Example

Enid, a 40-year-old single woman, is making a great deal of progress in terms of controlling her drinking through her involvement with an AA program. In terms of the managing her drinking, she is on the transition arrow of the helping model. But she is just deciding what she wants to do about a troubled relationship with a man. In fact, her drinking was, in part, an ineffective way of avoiding the problems in the relationship. She knows that she no longer wants to tolerate the psychological abuse she has been getting from him, but she also fears the vacuum she will create by cutting the relationship off. She is, therefore, trying to develop some preferred-scenario possibilities for a better relationship. She also realizes that ending the relationship might be the best option. Because of counseling, she has been much more assertive in the relationship. She now cuts off contact whenever he becomes abusive. That is, she is engaging in a series of "small acts" that help her better manage her life and discover further possibilities. Finally, since this is not the only time she has experienced psychological abuse, she is beginning to wonder what it is about herself that in some way almost draws contempt. She has a sneaking feeling that the contempt of others might merely mirror the way she feels about herself. She has also begun to wonder why she has stayed in a safe but low-paying job so long. She realizes that at work she is simply taken for granted. In other words, there are some issues that she has yet to explore.

In summary, because Enid has a troubled relationship with herself, she is likely to have troubled relationships with others, in this case her male friend. She probably resorts to drinking to "manage" her relationships both to herself and to others. It is an ineffective management technique, providing temporary relief from pain but, in the long run, causing even more pain.

Over the course of two years, the counselor helps Enid develop human resources for both support and challenge.

* She moves from one-to-one counseling to group counseling with occasional one-to-one sessions. Group members provide a great deal of both support and challenge.
* She begins attending church. In the church she attends a group something like Alcoholics Anonymous.
* Through one of the church groups she meets and develops a friendship with a 50-year-old woman who has "seen a lot of life" herself. She challenged Enid when she began feeling sorry for herself. She also introduced Enid to the world of art.
* She does some volunteer work at an AIDS center. The work challenges her and there is a great deal of camaraderie among the volunteers.

Since one of Enid's problems is that she is "out of community," these human resources constitute part of the "solution." Rather, all these contacts give her multiple opportunities to get back into community and both give and get support and challenge.

1. Summarize some goal you are pursuing and the action plan you have developed to get you there.
2. Identify the human resources that are already part of that plan.
3. Indicate the ways in which people provide support for you as you implement your plan.

4. Indicate ways in which people challenge you to keep to your plan or even change it when appropriate.

5. What further support and challenge would help you stick to your program?

6. Indicate ways of tapping into or developing the people resources needed to provide that support and challenge.

a. Summarize your goal and action plan.

_____

_____

_____

_____

_____

b. Identify the human resources that are already part of that plan.

_____

_____

_____

c. Indicate the ways in which people provide support for you as you implement your plan. How effectively do you tap into the support that is available?

_____

_____

_____

_____

_____

d. Indicate ways in which people challenge you to keep to your plan or even change it when appropriate. How effectively do you go out and seek the kind of challenge that will help you stay on course?

_____

_____

_____

e. What further support and challenge would help you stick to your program? What can you do to tap into or provide the human resources needed to do so?

_____

_____

_____

_____

_____

7. Share what you are learning through this exercise with a fellow trainee. Using empathy, probes, and challenge, help one another identify ways of using people more effectively to provide both support and challenge for your action plans.

EXERCISE 80: FAILURE TO USE THE PRINCIPLES OF BEHAVIOR

In your text review the principles of behavior as they apply to the implementation of programs (even better, study these principles much more thoroughly in Watson & Tharp's **SELF-DIRECTED BEHAVIOR**, Brooks/Cole, 1989). It seems that many programs fail because people ignore or misuse the principles and procedures related to incentives and rewards, extinction, punishment, and avoidance. In this exercise you are asked (a) to review some simple cases in which misuse of these principles contributed to the failure of a client's action program and (b) to indicate how these principles might have been used to help the action plan succeed.

* **Incentives and rewards.** Were there sufficient rewards or incentives for engaging in the program itself and in each of the steps of the program?

Corina wanted to graduate from college and then build a career. She was intelligent, but performed at only an average level in high school. Studies had never become that important for her. In college, each time she sat down with a text or a written assignment, she was in agony. She was in misery because she could no longer bluff her way through. Sheer will power got her through the first three semesters of college but it became too much for her and she quit.

What role might incentives and rewards have played?_____

_____

_____

_____

_____

_____

* **Extinction.** Were the effects of extinction ignored?

Lily wanted to read more serious books than her usual paperback novels. She realized that at first she would probably not find that kind of reading as rewarding (exciting) as she found pulp novels. She neither rewarded herself when she did read a serious book nor did she punish herself when she failed to read a serious book that she had intended to read. At the end of a year she found she had read only one serious book and part of a second. Her plan to engage in serious reading simply extinguished.

166

What might she have done to manage this extinction process?

_____

_____

_____

_____

_____

* **Punishment.** Was punishment misused as a motivator? Were the punitive side effects of action programs identified and   managed?

Perry was trying to lose weight. Whenever he ate more than his diet called for, he punished himself by calling off some social engagement he enjoyed. He thought that this kind of "self-discipline" was just what he needed. This disrupted his social life, punished his friends, and made him feel isolated. When he felt isolated, he tended to compensate by eating.

What might he have done to avoid the negative consequences of punishment?

_____

_____

_____

_____

* **Avoidance.** Were there more rewards for <u>not</u> engaging in the action program or any part of it than for engaging in it?

Terry, an AIDS patient, wanted to work on reconciliation with his family. He moved back to his home town and found a place to live and some supportive resources. However, often when he was about to engage in some reconciliation activity such as a visit to his parents or a lunch with a brother, some opportunity to do something with people in his new community of friends proved more inviting. For instance, he would visit a dying AIDS patient rather than his parents. Thus he avoided the pain of the visit home and substituted an activity he found rewarding.

What might Terry have done to manage his avoidance? _____

_____

_____

_____

_____

_____

In this exercise and the one that follows, it is important to remember that you are merely skimming the surface of the principles of human behavior. Further study of these principles, coupled with common-sense usage, will enable you to weave them instinctively into your interactions with your clients.

EXERCISE 81: PUTTING THE PRINCIPLES OF BEHAVIOR TO USE

In this exercise you are asked to use the principles of behavior to bolster programs you are currently engaged in or are about to undertake.

Situation #1

Briefly describe the goal or subgoal you are trying to achieve and the principal elements of the plan you have formulated to reach your goal.

_____

_____

_____

_____

_____

a. What incentives and rewards will help you raise the probability of your engaging effectively in the program?

_____

_____

_____

b. How can you apply the principle of <u>extinction</u> in a way that will raise the probability of your sticking to the plan?

_____

_____

_____

c. How can you apply what you know about <u>punishment</u> in a way that will raise the probability of your carrying our your plan?

_____

_____

_____

d. How can you use what you know about <u>avoidance</u> to help yourself engage in your plan as fully as possible?

_____

_____

_____

Situation #2

Briefly describe another goal or subgoal you are trying to achieve and the principal elements of the plan you have designed to achieve it.

_____

_____

_____

_____

a. What incentives and rewards will help you raise the probability of your engaging effectively in the program?

_____

_____

_____

b. How can you apply the principle of <u>extinction</u> in a way that will raise the probability of your sticking to the plan?

_____

_____

_____

c. How can you apply what you know about <u>punishment</u> in a way that will raise the probability of your carrying our your plan?

_____

_____

_____

d. How can you use what you know about <u>avoidance</u> to help yourself engage in your plan as fully as possible?

_____

_____

One of the main reasons problem-management and opportunity-development programs fail is that they are not monitored. Participation in a program slacks off sometimes without even being noticed. Entropy takes its toll. This means that monitoring has not been built into the program itself.

1. Use the following questions on monitoring to examine an action program in which you are currently engaged. An example accompanies each question.

a. **Involvement.** Are you participating or not?

Client. "I checked with the doctor and set up a reasonable diet but, to tell the truth, I haven't started it yet. I've been more or less just trying to cut down on what I eat."
Helper. "With what kind of results?"
Client. "I'm not sure. I haven't really checked."

b. **Degree of involvement.** If you are participating, how fully are you participating? What are you doing? What are you failing to do?

Todd and Sue had agreed to talk out petty annoyances with each other instead of saving them. Sue lived up to the agreement except when she felt hurt. Todd lived up to the agreement only when it was a question of "major" annoyances. Therefore, neither was participating fully in the action program. Although they were doing better than before, both were still saving up petty annoyances that they "cashed in" later in the form of some kind of blow up.

c. **Monitoring.** In what ways is monitoring built into the program itself? How can key people be tapped for feedback?

The staff at the rehabilitation center had weekly conferences with Roberta to discuss her progress in the physical therapy part of the rehabilitation program. Individual therapists kept her informed of the strengths and weaknesses of her participation. She monitored her psychological progress through weekly meetings with a counselor. She reviewed with him the tasks she had set herself in the previous meeting. For instance, she discussed her tendency to engage in self-defeating self-talk. Each day she filled out a check list to make sure that she was keeping to schedule. Effective monitoring had been built into this program.

d. **Progress indicators.** Are there some clear indications that, by implementing your plan, you are moving toward your goal or subgoal? What are these indications?

Despite the fact that neither was fulfilling the action-program contract fully, Sue and Todd discovered that the number of fights and arguments per week was actually diminishing. They also discovered that the fights they did have were not as bitter as they used to be. They were fighting more fairly with each other. This was clear because name-calling and the degree of bitterness that often permeated their fights had been greatly reduced.

e. **Changes in plan.** To what degree does your monitoring indicate that some changes in the plan are called for? What changes would make sense?

Beatrice was slacking off on a physical-fitness regimen that was part of an overall cardiac-disease prevention program. She thought she was lazy or "unmotivated." In discussing this with a counselor, she discovered that she had set the tempo too high. She was giving up because she was pushing herself too hard. After resetting her schedule, she had no difficulty fulfilling the requirements of the program.

f. **Link to original problem.** If the goal has been totally or even partially achieved, has it led to or is it leading to some kind of effective management of the original problem situation?

Jason's presenting complaint was a "poor self-image." This included feeling bad about his personal appearance. Since he was severely overweight, one goal was weight loss. He participated successfully in a weight-loss program. When he lost a fair amount of weight, he began to feel better about himself in two ways. He felt better about his physical appearance and he now saw himself as an agent in life rather than a victim. He felt good about himself because he could change things. He was on his way to handling his "poor self-image."

g. **Changes in goal.** Does your monitoring indicate that more fundamental changes are called for in the goal or agenda itself? This is more fundamental than changing the strategy or plan. Perhaps one or more goals are inappropriate, or set too high, or set too low.

Karen set a goal of re-setting a relationship with a male friend. She had no intention of marrying him and therefore wanted to step back from the kinds of intimacy she associated with marriage. After a four-month moratorium in their relationship to which they had both agreed, they began seeing each other as "just friends." Informal monitoring indicated that he wanted to be more than just friends and that she at times encouraged him. They both finally agreed to terminate their relationship. The goal of being just friends had proved unworkable.

h. **Recycling.** What kind of further recycling of the problem-management process might be useful at this point?

Once Todd and Sue got some of their fighting and bitterness under control, they were free to ask themselves, "What's really going on here?" In talking more civilly to each other, they discovered a number of issues: Todd was dissatisfied with his job but felt that he had to stick to it because it paid so well; Sue was working just to keep herself busy, but she had said nothing about a career because she and Todd had talked about the timing of a family. It was now time to use the helping process to focus on issues such as these.

Give a brief summary of your goal and action plan.

_____

_____

_____

_____

_____

a. **Participation.** Are you actually pursuing your plan? Did you ever start? Have you given up? Explain briefly.

_____

_____

_____

b. **Degree of participation.** To what degree are you implementing the plan? What are you doing? What are you failing to do?

_____

_____

_____

_____

_____

c. **Monitoring.** In what ways is monitoring built into the plan itself? If monitoring is not built in, what can you do to monitor your participation more effectively? What part can feedback from others play in the monitoring process?

_____

_____

_____

_____

d. **Progress indicators.** How do you know you are moving toward your goal? Give specific indications.

_____

_____

_____

_____

e. **Changes in plan.** Given what you have learned from monitoring, what changes, if any, are needed in your plan?

_____

_____

_____

_____

f. **Link to problem.** If your goal has been fully or even partially accomplished, has it led to or is it leading to some kind of effective management of the original problem situation or some part of it? How can you tell?

_____

_____

_____

_____

_____

g. **Modifications in goal.** What modifications, if any, do you have to make in your preferred-scenario goals?

_____

_____

_____

h. **Recycling.** What kind of further recycling of the problem-management process would be useful at this point?

_____

_____

_____

_____